CHILD REARING,
PERSONALITY DEVELOPMENT
AND DEVIANT BEHAVIOR

CHILD REARING, PERSONALITY DEVELOPMENT AND DEVIANT BEHAVIOR

**HUUB ANGENENT &
ANTON DE MAN**
Bishop's University

THOMPSON EDUCATIONAL PUBLISHING, INC

Orders may be sent to:

United States	or	*Canada*
240 Portage Road		11 Briarcroft Road
Lewiston, New York		Toronto, Ontario
14092		M6S 1H3

For faster delivery, please send your order by telephone or fax to:
Tel (416) 766–2763 / Fax (416) 766–0398

Cover photo: Courtesy of AIB, Ottawa.

Cataloguing in Publication Data
Angenent, Huub
    Child rearing, personality development & deviant behavior

Includes index.
ISBN 1-55077-040-3

1. Child rearing.   2. Personality development.
3. Deviant behavior.   I. De Man, A. F. (Anton Frans),
1947-   .   II. Title.

HQ769.A75   1993   305.23'1   C92-094722-0

1 2 3 4   95 94 93 92

Table of Contents

Preface

How parents raise a child very much determines the way in which the child's personality develops. Under the parents' influence, the child develops individual characteristics, internalizes specific norms and ideas, and begins to behave in particular ways. This holds for all child-rearing environments—the traditional family as well as alternative living arrangements.

This book is primarily about child rearing and personality development within the family. We therefore devote a considerable amount of attention to the family as a social agent and milieu for raising children. This is followed by discussion of general patterns of child rearing and personality development and the manner in which these patterns relate to each other. We subsequently review three forms of deviant behavior (aggression, juvenile delinquency and runaways) and the factors associated with each.

We intend this book as an overview, a frame of reference for both thought and practical application. It is aimed at those who wish to learn about children, childhood and child rearing.

1

DEVELOPMENT OF THE PERSONALITY IN THE FAMILY

MATURATION AND LEARNING

Both internal maturational processes and external environmental influences determine human development. Children are born with genetically determined or congenitally organized response tendencies, which they use to interact with their environment. As they grow older, their physical, social and psychological environments gradually expand bringing about changes in their behavior. Thus, their development results from the interaction of forces and influences that emerge from within themselves (*maturation*) and from outside themselves (*learning*). These forces and influences mix, however, and it is often difficult to separate the contributions of maturation and learning to overall development.

Initially, young children demonstrate a limited number of inborn reactions, such as sucking, swallowing, moving and making noises. Over time, these tendencies differentiate into biological and social needs. Biological needs are primarily aimed at obtaining satisfaction (for example, an infant will cry when hungry and feel satisfied when fed), whereas social needs are oriented toward developing and maintaining interpersonal relationships (e.g., the need for company). Gradually, behavior becomes a mixture of biological and social activities. For example, infants soon associate eating not only with the satisfaction of a biological need but also with maintaining personal contact with their mother.

Development progresses through maturational stages that are more or less the same for everybody and thus relatively predictable. Although all children progress through approximately the same developmental stages, they do so in their own way and at their own speed. Eating, sleeping and toilet behavior, as well as cognition and language development, are examples of internally motivated stages.

Generally, a child's development progresses from being dependent and socially aloof to being independent and socially involved. However, development is not invariably linear. Each developmental level has its positive and negative aspects, and sometimes development regresses. Stages during which the child is optimally adjusted, enjoys good contact with the environment and develops progressively may give way to periods of personal and social crisis. Stages characterized by balance alternate on a more or less predictable basis with periods characterized by disharmony, a phenomenon particularly noticeable in young children.

Infancy, childhood and adolescence are unique periods of life because of the rapid changes that take place at the biological as well as the socio-psychological level. With respect to the latter, it may be noted that a need for close social ties manifests itself already during the early years and continues throughout life. Social relationships that involve deep, intense contacts are highly satisfying and crucial to healthy development and adjustment. Relationships of this nature are most often found in small groups, particularly those that provide people with a sense of belonging and identity. Such groups are referred to as *primary groups*, as opposed to the larger, less cohesive *secondary groups,* in which members may feel alienated or lonely.

In many cultures, the family is the most prominent primary group. The term *family* refers to a group comprised of children and one or two adults (married or not). The adults may be the natural parents or foster or adoptive parents. It is a community of relatively stable and lasting nature, whose members experience and accomplish things together. Feelings of belonging, togetherness and mutual responsibility form its basis.

The family plays an important role in a child's personality development. It is the setting where youngsters develop a large part of their identity, self-image, self-esteem and self-ideal. They learn how to interact with others, learn what is right and wrong, and how to behave accordingly, and they internalize conventional norms and customs. Although the social circle of the children is gradually extended beyond the immediate family environment, interactions within the family are crucial influences on development. These contacts are the first and most often the only ones children have on a continuing basis, especially during their early years.

Within the family, the relationship with the *parents* is of particular importance. Parents model and communicate values, rules, traditions and knowledge, and this facilitates the personal development and social adaptation of their youngsters. Elders contribute to the assumptions children make about themselves, the world and their relationships to that world. As agents of society, parents prepare their children to take their place in the community. More than anyone, they are aware of the activities of their children and thus are in a position to guide and supervise them and protect them from getting into trouble. Should the latter nevertheless happen, it is the parents who are in the best position to take corrective actions to solve the problem.

It is for these reasons that parent-child relationships have such a decisive influence on the personality development of children. These relationships, if positive, foster the acquisition of perceptions, cognitions and values that allow children to view themselves as independent individuals who are aware of their strengths and weaknesses and have no difficulty interacting with others.

MOTHER AND CHILD

Infants initially do not differentiate between what is a part of them and what is not. They probably perceive all experience, whether produced by internal sensations or external agents, as unitary. Only gradually will they learn to distinguish between that which is part of them and that which is external. It is this differentiation that leads to the development of a *self-concept*.

Ordinarily, the first interpersonal contact children establish is with the mother, who satisfies their basic needs. For many years, the development of their personality takes place under her direct influence. Mother and child develop an intense relationship, which leaves the child sensitive to the emotions of the mother and vice versa.

The way the mother feels about the child is particularly important to the latter. If the child receives positive feedback, such as warmth, security and acceptance, he or she will experience satisfaction and happiness. Negative feedback such as coldness, rejection, hostility, and lack of respect, will make the child unhappy. Over time, the child comes to evaluate positively those behaviors that lead to positive feedback from the mother and negatively those that generate negative responses. The child will then display those positively evaluated behaviors and incorporate them into his or her self-concept, whereas the child will tend to cease those behaviors of which the mother disapproves. In later years, the child will assimilate only experiences that are consistent with the existing self-concept. Experiences that run in opposition to this concept may be perceptually distorted to make them acceptable, or, if this is not possible, rejected.

As the child grows older, the self-concept becomes more and more independent. The importance of the mother as example diminishes, and the child establishes significant social relationships with other people. These relationships with other family members and subsequently with individuals outside the immediate family circle in turn contribute to the development of the child's personality.

FATHER AND CHILD

Particularly during the early years, the father-child relationship is much less intimate than the one between mother and child. Young children focus their attention on the mother and turn to her when they encounter difficulties. Their relationship with her is generally more intense, delicate, sensitive and vulnerable than that with their father. In most families, the father-child relationship is more strained and less comfortable. The father often is seen as the disciplinarian, unlike the mother, who is perceived as having a nurturing role.

The contribution of the father to the child-rearing process is essential, but—because of culturally determined circumstances — often less extensive in nature, particularly during the early years. The father tends to become more important when the child is about three years old. Initially, children, particularly girls, may perceive the father as an object of admiration and favor him over the mother. Soon he becomes the great authority on whom the child blindly relies, both inside the home as well as outside. This reaches a peak when the child is about four years old. By the age of five, the child tends to return to the mother. However, the father's authority remains important to subsequent development, although the child may occasionally test his authority. Real challenge of the parents does not take place until the child reaches puberty. By the time the child reaches the age of ten and is capable of more mature contact, the father's influence once again gains in importance.

The literature on child rearing—especially the early literature—suggests that the mother plays the most important role in child rearing, whereas the father's contribution is of secondary importance. It is true that in Western cultures the mother traditionally has been more intensely involved with the children, particularly during the early years. However, especially as the child grows older, the father begins to make significant contributions. Early studies of the contributions of mothers and fathers to the child-rearing process appear to have approached the question in a biased manner and therefore have underestimated the role of the father. More recent investigations have shown that the latter is more important to the child and the socialization process than previously thought. The child's social behavior is very much influenced by the father's opinions and example. Furthermore, the paternal influence has increased with the current trend for parents to raise children together. Fathers assume parental responsibilities that society traditionally assigned to mothers and vice versa. As a result, fathers have become more involved with their children.

THE GROWING CHILD

The older the children, the more their personality development is influenced by persons outside the family (e.g., grandparents, neighbors, teachers, friends and peers). When they start school, they come in contact with teachers and fellow students, who each in their own specific way will play an important role in their social development. Teachers will encourage them to broaden their horizons and assist them in adjusting to a multitude of new rules and regulations. They will learn competition, compromise and cooperation. Also, the influence of friends and peers is powerful. The need for contact with age mates is already evident during childhood, but peers assume a more central role when the child reaches the age of nine. Parents may get the impression that their children only come home to eat and sleep. Film stars and pop idols also exert a large—though temporary—influence on children during puberty.

Adolescence is characterized by a search for identity. The children begin to experience themselves as individual personalities and develop a sense of self. They begin to see themselves as unique individuals, with their own ideals and ideas, value systems, personal lifestyles, expectations for the future and place in society.

Identity development is a necessary preparation for the psychological maturity and independence of adulthood. A well-established identity is a prerequisite for successful functioning in life. Failure to establish a clear identity may lead to social isolation, feelings of meaninglessness and lack of intimacy during adulthood. People who successfully establish their identity, on the other hand, will be able to enter relationships with others that are characterized by cooperation and affiliation.

Parents play an important role in this process, first by modeling values and thereby influencing the ultimate identity of their children. A good parent-child relationship may promote a harmonious course of development.

The development of an identity influences the manner in which children orient themselves toward the world. The child abandons the concrete attitudes of childhood and adopts an interest in general life values and abstract problems, such as the environment, discrimination, war and peace. Social concerns rapidly develop, and children have intense contact with peers, with whom they establish intimate and lasting relationships. The children begin to view themselves as belonging to specific groups and, ultimately, as members of society. Real social life begins in adolescence.

Because of the many changes and uncertainties that confront children during adolescence, this period of life tends to be somewhat erratic. Nevertheless, only a small minority of adolescents experience it as a stormy period characterized by conflict and identity crises. Most use adolescence to experiment and in time develop their own identity. As a result, they ultimately can function in a mature manner in marriage and society.

An important consequence of identity development is that children begin to behave more independently. They previously relied on their parents and blindly adopted their norms and customs, but now they begin to act more autonomously. They question and discuss many of the ideas, beliefs and habits of the parents. Their family link loses its exclusive character, and people other than the parents—particularly friends and peers—begin to exert an increasing influence.

The changed attitudes of the adolescents and their greater independence from their parents may lead to all sorts of differences in opinion between elders and children, a phenomenon referred to by some as *generation conflict*. This term implies that children often have fierce but normal confrontations with their parents related to their process of gaining independence. However, the generation conflict—a favorite subject with the news media—is largely a myth. Although adolescents increasingly disagree with their parents, most get along quite well with them. Parents and children generally do not reject one another, and the disagreements seldom lead to a split. On the contrary, between them is usually a great deal of solidarity and loyalty.

Even during adulthood, the influence of the parents and the home continues to play an important role. However, the process of becoming autonomous continues and this influence diminishes over time. Parents and other family members face increasing competition from friends, peers, colleagues and particularly from the families the young adults themselves establish. The circle closes and the process starts anew.

2

THE CHILD AND THE FAMILY: HISTORICAL PERSPECTIVES

SOCIETY, FAMILY, CHILDREN, AND CHILD REARING

The family as a basic social unit is a time-honored institution that has undergone many changes in the course of history. Because it is an institution very much influenced by contemporary ways of thinking, its place and function in society have always been and always will be subject to change. In other words: different times, different manners; different times, different families.

In the past, the family was a basic social unit that assumed a multitude of roles. The household was a conjugal as well as an economic unit. It was at the center of property relations and handled certain kinds of judicial problems. Relatives played a peacekeeping role and, in the absence of organized police forces, family discipline was an important insurance against disorder. Kinship also was important in political affairs, forming centers of organization for competing factions and interest groups. Over the centuries, these roles have gradually changed. The family has relinquished a number of tasks and now is sharing many responsibilities with other institutions. Nevertheless, it remains a particularly influential force in society, especially because it is the earliest and most significant agent of socialization.

In the same way that social conditions affect a family's function, so they affect child rearing. Developments in society and the ensuing modifications in the family's place and function do not leave internal family relations untouched. This has repercussions for the child-rearing process, the purpose and format of which are constantly subject to change. As a result, child-rearing approaches differ from generation to generation.

In the past, children tended to occupy a subordinate position in families and to be dominated by autocratic parents. They had no rights and were controlled and often exploited by their elders. Over the centuries, however, their individuality, rights and uniqueness have been more and more recognized, even to the point that today's society could be considered child-centered. This chapter will briefly review some of the historical, religious, political, philosophical and scientific factors in the development of the family, children and child rearing.

THE MIDDLE AGES

In medieval Western Europe, society did not regard childhood as an important, separate stage of life during which children pass through a series of qualitative changes. The idea that human beings are the product of instantaneous creation—and not, as is assumed by many today, of an extended evolutionary and developmental process—resulted in the perception of children as differing from adults only in quantitative terms. Parents realized that the very young required some care and attention to survive; but as soon as they were old enough to look after themselves, they were included in the adult world, although in a subordinate position. Because children became part of the adult world at such an early age, they were not as childlike as children are today and childhood as it is known now did not exist.

By present standards, parents in those days regarded their children with indifference. This indifference may have stemmed from the demographic characteristics of the Middle Ages. Birth control and medical care had not yet reached a high level of effectiveness. There were high birth rates, along with high mortality rates during childbirth and still higher mortality rates for infants. It is therefore not surprising that society considered children replaceable and of limited importance. Physical survival appears to have been the dominant issue in child rearing—parents were not so much concerned with methods of child rearing as with whether they would able to raise their children at all. So many children died of natural causes at an early age that parents quite likely were afraid to form strong attachments to their infants until they were satisfied that their children would survive.

The biblical view of human nature also left its mark on the quality of the parent-child relationship. It was thought that children were born with an innate tendency toward wickedness that, unless suppressed, would grow stronger as they grew older. To limit the potentially undesirable consequences of this natural inclination, parents relied heavily on strict guidance and severe physical discipline.

Generally, life was harsh for the young ones. Even though parents certainly must have felt affection for their surviving children, the general atmosphere was not a warm and loving one. The level of child care was low, and adults often beat, terrorized or abused their children. A large number fell victim to neglect, abandonment, exposure and even infanticide because poverty, famine and disease rendered their parents either unable or unwilling to provide for them.

CHANGE IN ATTITUDES

Over the ages, significant changes have occurred in our thinking about children, childhood and child rearing. Parents became more aware of the special needs of the young and began taking their unique features into consideration. They recognized childhood as an important stage of life rather than a fast-passing period of transition. Several ideological, social and economic factors contributed to these changes.

Above all, a more democratic attitude emerged. Medieval society had been characterized by authority—the authority of the church, the feudal system, the economic order and the older generation. In the family, the father was provider, protector and—not least—ruler. Children in the household were very much dominated by his authority. The emancipation of children to the status they hold today was possible because of a general democratization of society, a process that marked its beginning in the Renaissance. Gradually, religious authority decayed, the rigid class system declined, the economic order changed and parental authority waned. The change in attitude toward children was a natural consequence of democratization, which recognized the idea of equal sovereignty, affirmed the dignity of the individual, favored reciprocity in parent-child relationships and encouraged more humane discipline.

Furthermore, the Renaissance marked the beginning of a revolt against church domination. In medieval times, the Christian tradition had a considerable influence on the prevailing attitudes toward children and child rearing. However, society increasingly criticized church dogma and clerical practice, and by the beginning of the sixteenth century, its various dissatisfactions culminated in the Protestant Reformation. The moral influence of the Reformation and subsequent Counter-Reformation brought about a change in mentality with respect to children. People began to view childhood as an innocent, unspoiled period of life to be maintained for an extended period and safeguarded against external pollution.

THE PHILOSOPHERS

As part of the historical developments, leading intellectuals began to discuss the nature of childhood and the preferred ways of raising children. As interest in the child spread rather widely, and children came to be valued more highly, increasingly they were recognized as autonomous individuals and acknowledged for their special child-like nature.

Locke

In classical times, Plato suggested that the acquisition of knowledge is merely a process of remembering ideas that the soul had observed during its pre-existence and latently brought along at birth. Similarly, during the Middle Ages the educational objective was to bring forth innate, God-given ideas. John Locke, the leading philosopher of the Enlightenment and founder of this theory of education, held a viewpoint that was an antithesis to these earlier beliefs. Although he accepted inborn individual differences in intelligence and temperament, he rejected the doctrine of innate ideas. Instead, he proposed that the mind of the newborn is a *tabula rasa*—a blank slate—and that all knowledge comes from experience.

The *tabula rasa* concept implies that children are fundamentally different from adults and assigns great importance to the developmental years, during which the child is susceptible to many influences. Moreover, it attributes great power to parents, who can shape their children's development by manipulating environmental circumstances. Because it assumed that one could teach children almost anything, this viewpoint resulted in an optimistic approach to education. According to Locke, not only should parents serve as teachers, but to teach effectively they should command the respect and affection of their children. If they are to achieve this, they must not rely on physical punishment, a method of control still used by many parents of that time. Locke felt that severe punishment would inflict great harm in education, and he called for a change in disciplinary practices. He suggested that reasoning with the child and setting a good example were the best child-rearing methods. Noting that children were sensitive to recognition, he proposed that through praise, commendation and relying on children's sense of honor, parents could exert great influence over the future behavior of their children.

Rousseau

Jean-Jacques Rousseau also proposed radical revisions in contemporary thought about children. His influence has been extensive. Not only may he be considered the most important educator of the Enlightenment, but his ideas also influenced virtually every theory of education in the ensuing centuries. Rousseau suggested that children are basically good but are corrupted by bad education and by the demands, restrictions, limitations and rigid discipline that adult society imposes on them. He felt that to avoid their corruption and to foster their natural goodness, society should protect children against negative influences.

Rousseau thought that many parents do not realize that children have their own unique way of observing, thinking and feeling. He noted that childhood is an important developmental stage, with its own behaviors consistent with the demands of that period of life. He felt that young children should not be encouraged to replace these behaviors with adult ways of functioning. He suggested that developmental events have a natural order, and that the good tendencies present at birth should be allowed to develop naturally in a relatively unrestricted environment. Children should learn through their own experiences and only when they desire to do so. They are not passive recipients but rather engage in their environment and select from it what they need for each stage of their development. They themselves know what can or cannot be done and instinctively strive for what is good. Spontaneity must be central to child rearing. The self-directed activities of children lead to an increasing independence, whereas their initial self-centered emotionality evolves into an altruistic attitude toward life. Children have no absolute need for a great deal of adult supervision and should be allowed to grow as their nature dictates, not as prescribed by their parents. Reward and punishment and demanding obedience are not good child-rearing methods. Children do not learn because of force but because they are convinced that something either should be or is necessary.

Rousseau's words should not be interpreted to mean that he advocated total permissiveness in child rearing. He rather proposed freedom within clearly articulated boundaries—a kind of neutral control brought about by the setting of inalterable limits. Rousseau thought that children are quite capable of determining these limits for themselves and thus should be exposed to as little parental pressure and guidance as possible.

CHANGES IN FAMILY TYPES

The underlying developments that were expressed most clearly in the ideas of Locke and Rousseau continued during the ensuing centuries. Significant in this process was the decline in the number of large families and the change in the structure and functioning of the household.

During the Middle Ages, birth and mortality rates were extremely high, but around the middle of the eighteenth century the mortality rate declined while population figures increased. The birth rate remained high until the latter half of the nineteenth century, when it also began to decline. These developments coincided with a rapid change toward industrialization and urbanization. Industrialization created a new economic system that, with its threats of irregular employment and unemployment, meant insecurity for many workers. This insecurity may have been a motivating factor in the decision to limit family size. Urbanization may have been another. Formerly, children were a family asset as laborers. Put to work at an early age, they were a source of income to their parents. As society moved from a rural-agricultural economy to an urban-industrial economy, the opportunities for early, gradual employment of the young—so prevalent in rural society—diminished. Moreover, with the introduction of compulsory education, children became even more of a family liability. Thus, with the decline of the large family, smaller numbers of children permitted closer contact between parents and children and a corresponding change in their relationship.

Besides the decrease in average family size, there were other changes in family structure and function. As a result, new types of families evolved. In previous centuries, the nuclear family was embedded in the extended family, where it was surrounded and influenced by several social institutions, such as class, church and neighborhood. Because of its subsidiary position, the nuclear family had neither existence by itself nor value in itself; external factors largely determined effective family functioning. Hence, the family focused on communal goals dictated by relatives and by society in general. Because of this orientation, the family could be labeled *outer-directed.*

Over time, the family freed itself from its often oppressive ties with relatives and social institutions. It became an independent institution and gained in intrinsic value and meaning. During this process, which we call the *first emancipation,* the emphasis shifted to personal relationships within the family. As a result, the family evolved into a rather closed little world with a limited horizon. This closed family, which tended to be relatively large, still had a rather authoritarian structure, with the father, as head, maintaining rigid discipline. It isolated itself, set boundaries and generally became *inner-directed.*

This inner-directed orientation has come under attack, particularly during the past few decades. Increasingly, closeness has had to yield to openness. In this, what we call the *second emancipation,* the *open family* gradually replaced the *closed family*. The open family is relatively small and has more democratic internal relationships. It emphasizes togetherness and child rearing. The father is less authoritarian and the mother less of a pivotal force in family affairs than was the case in the closed family. It is increasingly oriented toward the environment and communication with society. These contacts are not like the rigid relationships prevalent before the first emancipation, which burdened the family with externally imposed, authoritarian guidelines. They are relationships in which family members interact with people from a variety of social backgrounds. The family has become *other-directed*.

This increasing openness goes both ways. That is, society concerns itself more with familial tasks and family members increasingly participate in social activities. Several tasks traditionally assigned to the family are assumed by other institutions, whereas family members participate more and more in a variety of external social activities. The family has been "socialized" in the sense that there is greater mutual interaction with society.

CHILD REARING IN NORTH AMERICA

As was the case in Europe, parents in North America increasingly became interested in matters related to child rearing. Early nineteenth century American literature suggests that three different attitudes toward children and child rearing prevailed at that time. The first was based on the doctrine of original sin, which states that Adam burdened humankind with a universal sinful condition by committing the first sin. It was thought that man is not a sinner because he sins, but rather that he sins because he is a sinner. Consequently, adherents of this philosophy viewed children as having an innate tendency toward wickedness that would grow stronger unless they received careful and strict guidance. To free children from the clutch of their evil nature, parents enforced absolute obedience to their demands.

The second philosophy centered around the belief that parents should harden their children and encourage natural behavior. It was thought that such an approach would ensure that young ones became strong, vigorous and unspoiled adults.

The third viewpoint suggested that children be led (not driven) and persuaded (not commanded). It considered corporal punishment undesirable, ineffective and damaging and instead emphasized the use of encouragement and reward. Children were regarded as having certain needs and potentials that parents were not to frustrate or control but rather to encourage and help fulfill. This viewpoint gained widespread acceptance later in the century.

By the end of the 19th century, American parents displayed great interest in the physical and personality development of their children. They were very much concerned with instilling solid moral character and attempted to do so by providing a good Christian atmosphere in the home. Although information on child rearing was available through various publications, parents of that period, unlike their modern counterparts, were not yet bombarded with scientific, pseudo-scientific and often conflicting information about every aspect of child development. This was the time when mother still knew best. Her maternal confidence was not yet shaken and she was not afraid to rely on her instincts. Motherhood and mother love were exalted as never before.

This exaltation continued into the early years of the present century. However, about 1910 a striking change in attitude emerged. Although society continued to emphasize the development of a good character, it advocated a more rigid approach to achieve this goal. The showering of love on children increasingly made way for an emphasis on discipline and strict scheduling.

This shift from a sentimental, indulgent attitude to one of regimentation and sternness did not parallel scientific developments. The behavioral scientists of that time did not provide experimental evidence supporting this change, and it appears that the authors who advocated strict child rearing were merely airing their own opinions. Nevertheless, these opinions may have had an important influence. The number of large households in which several generations lived under one roof had decreased. Previously child rearing had been simple and straightforward under the guidance of older, more experienced family members. Now, parents no longer had their traditional sources of advice and support. They therefore increasingly turned to people outside the family who claimed to possess special expertise.

EXPERTS ON CHILD REARING

Watson and Behaviorism

In the 1920s, Watsonian behaviorism gained in influence. Through his writings and voice in the Children's Bureau, John Watson promoted a view of child rearing that was characterized by extreme environmentalism. He apparently was not impressed by the ways that parents of his time were raising their children. He thought that traditional child rearing had been unsuccessful and that there were more scientific ways to raise children. He considered it the task of behaviorists to teach parents what constituted responsible child care.

Watson placed a heavy responsibility on the parents' shoulders. He rejected the view that children are the product of unfolding inborn characteristics, over which parents have little or no control. In advocating a highly controlled and structured child-rearing regime, he instead suggested that parents build in at an early age everything that is to appear later. By controlling the child's environment and training, parents would be able to mold their children to meet the behavioral standards set by their home and group. Should children deviate from these standards, their parents and every other individual who contributed to their development would be to blame.

Gesell and Maturation

In the 1930s and following decades, new ideas emerged from research in psychology, psychiatry, pediatrics and education that promoted a less-controlling attitude.

Maturation-oriented experts proposed that the techniques and procedures of child rearing be brought in line with the growth characteristics of the developing child. Arnold Gesell, for instance, opposed the behavioralists' emphasis on environment and alternatively suggested that people come into their increased capacities primarily through intrinsic growth. He agreed that children have great powers of learning, but he felt that the extent to which they could be conditioned would be limited because they are born with characteristics that influence and determine their experiences.

Gesell suggested that, although the environment provides the setting for growth, its actual contribution to the developmental process is minimal, because children will grow as their germ plasma directs, within wide variations in experience. Environmental forces support, affect and modify the process but do not generate it. Growth is a force that comes from within the child.

This viewpoint suggests that every child is born with characteristics that are in close harmony with nature. Unfortunately, society has its own characteristics and demands, which often are counter to those of the child. Parents often think that their child's natural characteristics should be harmonized with those of the social order and consequently adapt their child-rearing practices to achieve this goal. Because development depends on deep-seated, instinctive forces, underlying growth characteristics—rather than a sophisticated culture—should determine the techniques and procedures of child guidance, Gesell felt.

He thought that an inflexible approach to child rearing, based on an arbitrary cultural norm, would ignore individuality and irregular fluctuations in child development. Because children have a self-regulating mechanism that can only be modified to certain limits and grow on their own terms, parents should create an atmosphere in which self-regulation and self-adjustment is possible.

Freud and Fixation

Unlike Gesell and Watson, who emphasized opposing ends of the nature-nurture dimension, Sigmund Freud pictured children as very much in conflict. He thought that no matter how well-organized and carefully constructed their environments or how strong and creative their forces of growth, children inevitably must face a confrontation between their own wishes and the demands of their environment.

Even though Freud paid considerable attention to instinctual forces and biologically determined developmental stages, he never underestimated the influence of the environment. He suggested that psycho-sexual development depends to a large extent on the interactions of the child with significant others, such as the parents, and with the conditions present at the various stages. All of the child's experiences provide unique possibilities for gratification or frustration. All may have a significant influence on development because insufficient gratification or over-indulgence may lead to fixation at particular stages. If the fixation is substantial, the child may build his or her character structure around it.

Freud's emphasis on the effects of fixation led some adherents of his theory to extreme interpretations. These people were so impressed by the long-lasting effects of severe fixation that they zealously advocated permissiveness in child rearing. Parents were strongly advised not to interfere too much with their children's behavior because adverse influences could result in fixation and eventually neurosis. On the other hand, open, flexible child-rearing procedures geared to the needs of the children would free them from conflict and allow them to develop into well-adjusted adults.

Other Experts, from Dewey to Spock

John Dewey suggested that the first goal of child rearing should be to allow children to develop themselves by exploring their world. Children must learn by doing, within a free and autonomous environment. Child rearing must consider the individual abilities and interests of youngsters and build on their instincts, which form the basis for their actions.

Maria Montessori proposed that child rearing be based on the natural development of children. All children in principle have the capacity to educate themselves. Therefore, they must be permitted to develop freely through self-directed activities, and not through adult guidance. Child rearing is, in fact, developmental assistance geared to a child's individual character, developmental level and needs. In each developmental stage, children have certain internal needs that are strong enough to make them act in a goal-directed manner if the situation is favorable. If they engage in appropriate behavior, it gives them a good feeling and, under such circumstances, reward and punishment become superfluous.

Ellen Key stated that children themselves should establish the goals of child rearing, with parents interfering as little as possible with their development. Nature is the best teacher. Children's rights are central to her philosophy.

Alexander Neill, of the anti-authoritarian school of thought, proposed that children should grow up without limitations. They must have the freedom to act out their impulses. It would be wrong to tell them what to do; they have to decide for themselves how they wish to behave. Thus, children themselves must determine what clothes to wear, when to change their clothing, whether they will go to school and so forth.

Benjamin Spock's early writings reflected the anti-authoritarian approach as well as Freud's ideas regarding child development. (Spock's ideas were a popular version of Freud's more complex notions.) When Spock published *The Common Sense Book of Baby and Child Care*, the attitude of most parents toward child rearing was still fairly strict and inflexible. His book moved a generation of parents away from the influence of earlier child-care experts. In addition to making available a great deal of information about the somatic side of pediatrics, he advocated much freedom for children whose wishes and desires should be granted as much as possible. He fulminated against strict child rearing and wanted as few rules as possible. Spock's influence has been great. His books have been used by generations of parents all over America and Europe as "cookbooks" for child rearing. As such, his work contributed to the emergence of a relaxed approach to child rearing by promoting greater understanding of children and greater flexibility in their care.

His later contributions—apparently in response to the criticism that he had spoiled a generation of children through permissiveness—reflected a return to conservative values. He emphasized the need for parents to guide their children to some degree and advocated a certain level of parental discipline. He admitted that too much permissiveness could lead to problems for the child. Parents should model ideals and norms and try to transmit these to their children.

Spock is not alone in this thinking. Although his era was followed by one in which the anti-authoritarian approach could flourish, lately more and more parents are reconsidering permissiveness and opting for more controlling child-rearing practices. The pendulum is swinging back, but the question remains as to what effect this will have on the present generation of children.

CONTEMPORARY CHILD REARING

Modern society changes rapidly and so does contemporary child rearing. The latter involves, among other activities, providing children with an opportunity to prepare themselves for the future. However, what this future will look like is rather uncertain, and therefore it is difficult to formulate concrete child-rearing goals. Consequently, parents do not know what their goals should be in raising their children. In previous, more static times, the situation was different; elders could expect the future to be like the past. Because parents knew what the future would look like and what would be expected of their children, child rearing was largely determined. This is no longer the case. Child-rearing traditions, as shaped by social and cultural institutions, such as socio-economic status, church and neighborhood, have largely disappeared; and parents can rely less frequently on established norms and values when raising their children. Modern child rearing is oriented toward the future rather than the past. Children today must be raised in such a manner that they can fend for themselves in an uncertain tomorrow. They must learn to be creative and to adapt to new situations. They must learn to think for themselves, act independently and not allow themselves to be thrown off balance. Society's pluralistic character requires that children learn to live in a complex network of social relationships and play a role in many different milieus and at many different levels. Child rearing should be a preparation for this—and this is not an easy task.

Many individuals and agencies are involved in this preparation process. The parents, teachers, educators, psychologists and other experts all make contributions. Unfortunately, these people do not always agree about what course to follow and may make contradicting recommendations. At present, a lot of information is available on child rearing. The scientific literature, popular press and news media bombard people with advice. This information is not superfluous if one wants to inform oneself about a complicated matter such as child rearing. However, the sheer volume of information can be overwhelming—and thus counterproductive.

Society, theoretically, offers virtually unlimited possibilities but, in reality, it presents many restrictions. For instance, many different educational options may exist, but job opportunities may be insufficient in particular fields. Many study areas exist, but so do student quotas. Many children from lower socio-economic levels cannot afford a post-secondary education. This contrast between theoretical possibility and concrete reality may turn child rearing into an ambivalent affair.

Summarizing, one may conclude that developments in society may have created greater opportunities for children and child rearing. However, traditional certainties have decreased and life has grown more complicated. As a result, child rearing has become more complex.

3

THE FAMILY

THE FAMILY AS THE IDEAL ARRANGEMENT

The family occupies an important position in society. It has been described as the backbone of society, the core of the social structure, the cornerstone of society, the shock-absorber and psychological advocate of the community, the protector of emotional stability and intergenerational communicator of culture and cultural values. Many regard the family as the ideal social unit, to the extent that they dismiss all other social arrangements as inferior.

Although the family undoubtedly is an important social agent, its status as the ideal social grouping should be viewed in perspective, particularly in terms of *familial instability* and of *alternative living arrangements*. The family certainly has its share of troubles. Rather than being an ideal, serene environment, it may have problems that range from minor disagreements to major conflicts, and it may encourage situations that threaten some of its members. These problems are often, but not always, manageable. Furthermore, the nuclear family is only one of several possible living arrangements in our society. Many people opt for alternative arrangements: the childless family, the single-parent family, lat-relationships (living apart together or living alone together relationships), communes and so on.

THE TROUBLED FAMILY

Not all families function harmoniously. In some, one or more family members behave in such a way as to cause constant emotional upheaval. In others, one or both parents are no longer satisfied with the marital relationship and express their disappointment in hostile ways. Some families, because of internal shortcomings or severe environmental pressures, cannot cope with the ordinary demands of family living. Consequently, family and marriage counseling services have long waiting lists, and agencies such as child guidance centers, child welfare offices, youth advisory boards and the police are faced with many similar requests for help.

Family trouble may express itself in violence, aggressive behavior between family members that exceeds acceptable limits. Sometimes, the family is so troubled that it becomes virtually impossible to keep it together, and one or both parents file for divorce.

Violence in the Family

Family members normally maintain frequent and intense contact with each other. Hence, the family may be a source of understanding, acceptance, support and safety. However, family relationships may also be at the root of disagreements, misunderstandings, tensions and conflicts. Usually, such problems stay within acceptable limits because a basically positive atmosphere prevails in most families. However, in some families, the lack of such an atmosphere, combined with other negative circumstances, may result in violent behavior. This violence may express itself in different ways, such as child abuse, sexual abuse or abuse of a parent, spouse, sibling or grandparent.

Child Abuse

Child abuse refers to the mistreatment of children by their natural or substitute parents. The abuse may be physical or psychological or may involve chronic neglect of the child. In cases of physical abuse, a person responsible for the child intentionally and more or less regularly inflicts bodily injuries or traumas, thereby jeopardizing the victim's health, safety or development. Psychological abuse may consist of name-calling, nagging, belittling, making the child look like a fool and so forth. Neglect arises when parents or guardians chronically fail to provide their children with adequate nutrition, hygiene, protection and medical care or when they socially ignore them.

Precise statistics of the extent of child abuse are not readily available. The problem is probably more widespread than is generally believed because the children and parents involved, as well as many bystanders, do not dare or care to discuss the matter. Children may fear possible repercussions, parents may feel ashamed or dread losing face, bystanders may not want to get involved or fear being accused of having made false allegations. Complicating the matter is that a certain amount of physical discipline is tolerated in most families. It is often not easy to determine the point at which physical punishment becomes mistreatment.

Child abuse may come to light when people outside the child's immediate environment, such as doctors or teachers, notice that something is wrong. These cases, however, are usually limited to situations in which the abuse is severe and physical in nature. A neglected child's predicament may remain undetected. Detection, of course, is vitally important because the abuse may be repeated and grow worse over time.

Mistreatment may have short-term as well as long-term effects. Physical abuse may result in injuries that heal if proper medical care is provided, or the victim may be scarred for life, or, in extreme cases, the child may die. Besides physical harm, there may be psychological consequences, particularly if the child is subjected to repeated abuse. Severely neglected children similarly may experience physical and psychological damage.

With respect to physical abuse, there are critical ages at which children are more likely to be mistreated. The first stage is during the first three months of life, when many infants suffer colic and cry incessantly. The second danger period is between the ages of two and three, when children display initial opposition to their parents. The third critical stage is between the ages of nine and eleven, when puberty begins. Finally, parents mistreat many adolescents.

Children are more often neglected than physically abused. Unlike physical abuse, there are no specific age periods during which neglect is more likely to occur. It has been noted, however, that this kind of treatment increases during times of economic hardship for the family.

Generally, boys are more often physically punished during child rearing than are their sisters. Therefore, one might expect that boys would be more frequent victims of child abuse, particularly physical abuse. In reality, however, there is not much difference in the overall number of boys and girls who are physically abused, but there is a difference in the age levels at which such mistreatment occurs. That is, boys are more frequently the victim during their first six years of life, whereas girls seem to be in the majority after the age of eleven. One explanation may be that during the early years boys tend to be more difficult than girls and thus are more likely to provoke parental anger. Furthermore, after the age of eleven, they are more able and willing to defend themselves, something that may not be the case with girls or young women.

In most families, discipline and punishment traditionally have been the responsibility of the male parent. One might therefore expect a greater incidence of child abuse by fathers. In reality, however, it is more often the mother who displays this type of behavior. A possible explanation may be that the burden of child rearing generally falls on the mother in our culture. As a result, she is on a daily basis involved with the problems caused by her children. Sometimes, this leads to a great deal of frustration, which, in turn, may provoke her to act in an abusive manner.

Of course, many factors may contribute to child abuse—many of these found in the family situation itself. There are usually difficulties between the parents and often friction between the parents and the children. These problems may be prompted by ill health, problematic finances, unemployment, unpleasant living conditions and substance abuse. Also, some abusing parents struggle with personal problems or psychiatric disturbances. Child abuse may occur when parents, because of their own incompetence, are incapable of dealing with their children. Immature parents may be unready for parenthood or lack the necessary child-rearing skills. The latter problem may be intensified if there is no support system (family, friends or neighbors) available to provide assistance. Child abuse may also occur when children do not meet parental expectations concerning toilet training, eating habits, school achievement and so forth. Sometimes a parent may abuse a child because the child is not of the desired sex. That is, the parent may have wanted a son but instead received a daughter or vice versa. Many of the above problems may be compounded if the child was unwanted to begin with.

Sexual Abuse

Sexual abuse is a special form of child abuse by parents or other individuals who play parental roles. In most cases, such abuse concerns sexual activity involving a daughter and her natural father, stepfather, adoptive father, foster father or guardian. Sexual abuse of boys usually takes place outside the family unit.

When the relationship involves a girl, it may continue for a long time before she is able personally to put a stop to it or reveal the situation to other people. In some cases, the child feels ambivalent about the relationship; that is, she very much dislikes what the abuser is doing to her but simultaneously experiences feelings of attraction, dependency or pity for him. In other cases, she does not dare tell the terrible truth because she fears the possible consequences of such a revelation. The sexual relationship can last a very long time when the father forces the child to keep it a secret or when the mother acts as if nothing is happening and provides no support. For the child, this may mean years of loneliness, the burden of a dark secret and many distressing experiences.

Besides possible physical effects, such as vaginal pain, genital infection and unwanted pregnancy, there may be serious psychological damage. Sexual abuse usually overwhelms the child, who cannot cope with the ordeal and often tries to repress it. This may lead to repressed anxieties. Confused and suffering from self-blame, the child faces these troubles alone. Secrecy and shame often result in problems with sexual identity and interpersonal relationships. These traumas frequently appear during puberty and adolescence but may last a lifetime.

Parent Abuse

Parent abuse is the mistreatment of parents by their children. The perpetrators usually are boys over the age of eleven. Younger children may cause their parents a great deal of trouble and may act aggressively towards them, but they are not really capable of harming them, either physically or psychologically.

Abusive children do not hesitate to mistreat their parents when they do not get their way or when the parents do something with which they disagree. In some cases, there is not even a reason—the child may just feel like harassing and abusing the parents. Sometimes the abuser terrorizes the whole family, whereas in other cases he or she may focus attention on one of the parents, who often tries to keep it a secret from his or her partner.

It is difficult to determine whether parent abuse has increased over the years. There has been a decline in parental authority, particularly the authority of the father, the traditional authority figure. Children nowadays stand less in awe of their elders and perhaps are less inhibited in their aggression toward their parents.

Children who abuse their parents generally are difficult children to begin with. At a very young age, they already tend to be troublesome, short-tempered and demanding. They expect others to cater to their wishes but are not willing to reciprocate. They are self-centered and search for power, so that they can dominate their environment.

Spouse Abuse

The problem of *spouse abuse*—particularly wife abuse—became better known during the 1970s because of the women's movement. This focused attention on the role of women in society, with discussion centered on the subservient position of women both inside and outside the family. In this context, the abuse of women became a topic of concern within the women's movement and within society in general.

As is the case with child abuse, it is difficult to assess the extent of the problem accurately. It is likely that only a small proportion of cases become public. Many abused women remain silent, some try to excuse their partner's conduct, and some even defend the treatment they receive. That support groups for battered women are kept busy indicates that there is a genuine problem.

Although the discussion thus far has focused on men's abuse of women, this should not be taken to mean that the reverse does not ever happen. Although not much attention has been given to this type of spouse abuse, indications are that quite a number of men are abused by women.

Child abuse, sexual abuse, parent abuse and spouse abuse are not the only forms of family violence. Brothers and sisters also may abuse each other, and there have been reports of grandparent abuse. However, not much information about these problems is yet available.

There is a certain relationship among the various forms of family violence. Although each type can exist independently, family violence sometimes spreads like wild fire. Violence begets violence, and on occasion becomes part of the pattern of individual families over generations.

Divorce

A good relationships between the parents forms the basis for a solid family. If the parents no longer get along and decide to go their separate ways, the family ceases to exist. Reasons for divorce are highly personal. Many relationships end because one or both partners fall out of love or because the partners are no longer interested in each other or lack mutual respect, understanding or trust. Often communication is inadequate, and interpersonal contact has deteriorated to the extent that continuation of the marriage is no longer possible. Other reasons may be incompatible personalities or social status. One of the partners may have ascended the social ladder faster than the other. Other factors may be unsatisfactory sexual relationships, extramarital affairs and personal problems, such as neurosis, anxiety or depression.

In most industrial societies, the number of divorces has increased. This increase is related to various developments in society during the last few decades, such as changes in traditional standards or norms, the individualization of society and the emancipation of women. Through the news media and in everyday life, people increasingly meet individuals from different cultural backgrounds who adhere to a variety of dissimilar norms. Consequently, the general applicability of traditional standards has declined. Rules have become more flexible and vague, to the extent that some people may experience a loss of standards. As part of this development, norms pertaining to marriage and separation have become less rigid, and society has adopted a more tolerant attitude toward divorce.

Society has become more and more individualized; that is, the number of meaningful social contacts that people maintain has decreased, in part, because the groups and institutions that formerly played major roles in the lives of individuals (e.g., church and neighborhood) have lost importance. People have also become more self-oriented and tend to converge in smaller social circles, particularly the family. They seek care, protection, love, relaxation, entertainment, a sense of belonging and personal contacts within the family. This individualization has led to the perception that marriage is a private affair between two people and of no concern to others. Social control over marriage has declined. Nowadays, if the partners agree that they cannot salvage their troubled marriage, they may dissolve the arrangement—unlike in the past, when societal pressures more or less forced couples to remain together and keep up the facade.

The emancipation of women has played a role in this process. Within the relationship, women have become more outspoken and independent. They freely express their own opinions and are less willing to blindly accept those of their partner. This aspect of emancipation—or perhaps of the husband's lack of emancipation—may lead to conflict and ultimately divorce. Furthermore, with many women now entering the paid work force, more have become financially independent. The financial independence of employed women and the increased availability of material and legal support for those who are not employed has made it less urgent for women to remain in an unsatisfactory marriage.

Of course, divorce is not an easy experience. Prior to the separation, there usually is a difficult period during which the partners increasingly become aware that their marriage is not going to last. To accept this is not always easy. Sometimes, the couple tries in vain to save the relationship. In some cases, couples can arrange their divorce in an amicable atmosphere. In others, there may be major conflicts and mutual accusations.

Whatever the situation, the partners have to go through a difficult period during which their psychological stability is heavily taxed. Some become tense and irritable, whereas others repress the problem or experience despair. Besides the emotional stress, they may experience legal and financial problems that they do not understand or for which they are inadequately prepared. It is therefore essential that they receive adequate advice and assistance, support that may be provided by marriage counselors, social workers, lawyers and others.

The situation is more complicated when children are involved. Children, particularly when they are older, are very much aware of the conflicts and tensions that emerge during the months or years preceding the divorce. These events affect them, and they must cope in some way. Furthermore, the divorce itself means that they must give up familiar relationships and circumstances. One parent will leave the home, the family may move, the children may have to change schools, and they may have to say good-bye to their friends. The greatest tokens of security to disappear, however, are the trusted parent-to-parent and parent-to-child relationships. Because of these changes, the youngster may develop feelings of insecurity, especially with respect to the future. This insecurity means that they have to go through a very difficult period of life.

Children respond in different ways to the divorce of their parents. To some, the divorce is unacceptable and they try to deny or repress it. Others attempt to repair the rift between the parents by acting as a mediator. Some blame their parents, have no sympathy for the decision and feel abandoned. Others blame themselves, feeling that they have caused the divorce by being bad children.

Many children find it difficult to cope with the divorce of their parents. Some feel ashamed and try to keep it a secret. A large number displays behavior problems and needs professional help. The problems may be expressed in aggressive, anti-social or criminal behaviors or in withdrawal and depression. It should be noted that these problems are often transient in nature. They are a direct response to the divorce and usually disappear when circumstances calm down. Much depends on the manner in which the parents approach the children. Parents can help make the divorce experience relatively acceptable to their children, an event with which they can live. This requires that the parents deal with their children in a rational manner, explaining the circumstances surrounding the divorce and providing an opportunity to discuss its various aspects. This discussion should be geared to the child's level. Children should not be asked to form an opinion about matters for which they are not yet ready, and parents should not try to have them take sides. Conflicts of loyalty may emerge, especially in cases in which the child cannot choose between the mother or father.

Of course, children are often better off after a divorce. They no longer have to endure confrontations between the parents or the stress associated with these encounters. They may experience relief.

ALTERNATIVE LIVING ARRANGEMENTS

The Childless Marriage

Although the family is a universal phenomenon, it is not the only possible living arrangement. An alternative is the childless marriage. In these marriages, one may differentiate between couples who would like to have children but remain childless for reasons beyond their control and couples who intentionally decide that they do not want children.

Approximately 75 percent of couples who want to have children encounter no problems. In most of the remaining cases, a medical solution (e.g., hormones, artificial insemination, surgery or test-tube fertilization) is found. One in ten couples remain childless despite all efforts. The couples in this category often have difficulty coping with this fact. As their plans for the future fall by the wayside, they must restructure their lives and deal with the feeling that they have lost something essential. The partners often are willing to do almost anything to have a child. Conflicts between the partners may surface, and these may lead to depression, anxiety and somatic problems. The childless couple generally cannot count on much understanding from others because others frequently do not know how to handle the situation. This applies not only to family and friends but also to physicians and other care givers. Often the partners do not want to discuss the situation with others. As a result, the couple has to deal with the problem on their own. They may obtain some support by joining a self-help group, where they come in contact with others facing the same problem. Adoption may also provide a solution.

About one in ten marriages remains voluntarily childless. It is usually comprised of educated partners of higher socio-economic status who gain satisfaction from their work and have many hobbies and social interests. They may decide to remain childless because they do not want to take responsibility for bringing children into this world and raising them. They may feel there are already enough people on earth, many of whom live a less-than-enviable existence. Moreover, they do not view the future, with its potential for environmental and other disasters, with great optimism. Others do not wish to have children for financial reasons; raising children is expensive and this may mean that the parents have to deny themselves of material things, something they are not prepared to do. In some marriages, the partners think that children would limit their personal freedom and growth because raising children requires time, energy and giving up a certain amount of liberty. Partners would have less time for each other or for work, interests, hobbies, parties and so on. Child rearing is on occasion an exhausting business, and one is less mobile and more tied to a fixed schedule. These factors may lead to a couple's decision to remain childless.

The problems encountered by partners who voluntarily remain childless very much resemble those of couples who are unable to have children. They also cannot count on much understanding but are often subjected to other people's curiosity. It is for this reason that they avoid conversations about their childlessness, which may alienate them from their family and friends. Parents and others frequently disapprove of their situation, and people with children often are envious of their greater freedom of movement and material well-being.

The Single-Parent Family

In single-parent families, one of the parents—usually the father—is absent because of death, separation, divorce or family migration patterns or because the missing partner never really became part of the family. An example of the latter is the father who does not marry or live with the unwed mother of his child.

Although fathers are increasingly awarded custody—as a result of a recent shift in socio-cultural thought in the courts and the community—women head the majority of single-parent households. In the past, when sexual morality was more strict than it is today, society accused unwed mothers of having trespassed the realm of acceptable behavior and of raising children under less than optimal circumstances. At present, motherhood without marriage is less stigmatized, and single parenthood has become a more acceptable family form. Perhaps as a result of this greater acceptability, the number of women who want children but do not wish to marry or live with the father has increased.

Single-parent families tend to have more than their share of problems. Financially, they are generally around or below the poverty line and often have to rely on welfare for support. Child rearing also is not always trouble-free. Absence of adequate parental control may lead to behavioral problems within the family as well as delinquency outside it. At school, these children tend to achieve less, repeat grades more often and have a higher rate of absenteeism. A relatively large number become runaways. Problems are generally more common in families that have experienced divorce and less frequent in families in which one parent is deceased.

Of course, one has to be careful not to generalize too much. There are many single-parent families that function well, particularly in cases where the missing parent has been replaced by a substitute "parent" (e.g., Big Brothers, Big Sisters). What really matters is that the child feels safe and secure and that he or she has contact with adults who can be trusted.

Lat-Relationships

Some people want to have a partner but at the same time wish to live apart. These individuals may opt for a *lat-relationship* (living apart together or living alone together relationships). In such relationships, the partners spend part of their time alone and part of their time together. Each partner has specific ideas about how much time he or she wishes to be with the other and how much time he or she wishes to be alone—and the amount of time together ideally represents a compromise between the needs of both partners. In reality, problems may arise when the couple cannot agree on the exact distribution of their time. One partner may prefer the other's company, whereas the other may place a higher priority on privacy.

In a lat-relationship, the partners live apart and maintain their own homes. Sometimes there is some overlap between the two households when, often for financial considerations, they combine some activities (e.g., shopping for groceries). Their time together usually involves sharing interests, hobbies, leisure activities and vacations.

Communal Living

Communal living arrangements are reminiscent of the extended family of the past in which several adults and children lived under the same roof. The main difference is that some members of the communal group are not related through family ties. The goal of the arrangement resembles that of the nuclear family; namely, to create an environment in which one feels at home and can grow as a person. The members are interested in cooperating as a group and in establishing interpersonal relationships that facilitate mutual support. Sometimes, but not necessarily, the group comes into existence because its members are dissatisfied with the functioning of the traditional family, which they view as too limiting. More often, the participants are motivated by a need to be with other people. They do not want to live their life alone, or they find a relationship with only one partner too restrictive. Others join for economic or political reasons.

In communal arrangements, the members to varying degrees share living quarters, chores, food and, sometimes, finances. Income and property, however, seldom are really part of the collective domain. Children in the group have less exclusive claims on their parents, brothers and sisters. They grow up in the company of several other persons, to whom they may or may not be directly related. This may benefit their social development, but, on the other hand, they may not receive sufficient personal attention and therefore feel insecure.

Many of these arrangements fail because of personality differences. The members discover that differences in ideas, interests and temperament make it difficult to establish and maintain a relatively cohesive group. Moreover, people vary in their commitment to group participation. Some wish to keep a certain amount of privacy, an attitude that others may not appreciate. As a result, people may withdraw from the group. Sometimes, the arrangement falls apart because the members cannot agree on how to share the inevitable chores. Communal living arrangements generally do not survive very long. The average life span is considerably less than that of the average marriage.

Singles

Singles are unmarried individuals. They either have never been married or were part of a marriage that later dissolved. Singles, particularly those who have never been married, are often viewed in a stereotypical manner. They have the disadvantage of not fitting in with society's traditional expectation, which envisions that people are married or at least act as couples. Single men are perceived as swingers, egocentric, superficial or homosexual. Single women generally are viewed as bitter, jealous, maladapted, inhibited, asexual, masculine or opinionated. The term "old spinster" is not frequently used any more, but the concept has not yet disappeared.

More recently, society has regarded single life in a more positive manner. It is less frequently viewed as a last resort, when other ways of life are not possible, but as a consciously chosen and acceptable alternative. In fact, the number of single men and women has significantly increased, in part because of a rise in the divorce rate.

Singles are indeed alone in the sense that they spend much of their time by themselves and do many activities, such as household chores, hobbies and vacationing, on their own. Their quality of life has room for improvement. They are generally less happy than people who are married or live in common-law arrangements. They have more psychological and physical problems and tend to live shorter lives (often because of suicide or cardiac difficulties). Single men encounter more problems than single women. Divorced singles have more problems than singles who have never been married or those who have been widowed.

4

CHILD REARING IN THE FAMILY

FACTORS INFLUENCING CHILD REARING

The way parents raise their children depends on a variety of factors. General factors, those found in almost every family, include the mental and physical health of family members; the quality of the home environment (furnishings and general ambience); the degree of material care (food, shelter, drink and clothing); the way the household is managed (order and planning); family norms, values and aspirations; the emotional atmosphere (coherence, warmth); interpersonal relationships (acceptance, trust, support, under-standing); and life style (interests, hobbies). Besides these general factors, more specific variables influence some families. These may include, for instance, the death, illness, or behavior of a family member.

This book does not concern itself with specific factors but focuses its attention on general ones. These general factors are categorized into several groups; namely, *social factors* (education of the parents, family income, occupation of the father, employment of the mother, and socio-economic status), *personal factors* (the personality, age and gender of parents and children) and *family factors* (family size and birth order).

Social Factors

A family's child-rearing practices depend to a large extent on its social circumstances. With respect to the latter, one may distinguish two facets, one cultural and the other economic. These two aspects interrelate, and it is therefore difficult to define their individual influence on child rearing.

The cultural facet corresponds to the intellectual development of the parents which, in turn, is strongly related to educational level. That is, better educated people generally are more broadly developed intellectually than those who are less well-educated. The economic aspect directly relates to family income, which normally consists of the earnings of the parents. This income depends on the occupational level of the parents—the higher the occupational level, the better off the family is materially. This professional level, in turn, is affected by level of education—generally, the higher the level of education, the higher the professional level. Thus, a link can be established between the cultural and economic character of a child-rearing environment and education.

We will now discuss the various factors that play a role in this multifaceted network.

Education of the Parents

The educational background of the parents to a large extent determines the family's material status as well as its cultural and intellectual characteristics. Well-educated parents possess greater insight and knowledge and therefore are in a better position to understand what is and what is not possible in child rearing. They are more cognizant of what can be expected from children and less likely to be confronted with surprises. In general, they also know more about child-rearing methods and are better able to apply this knowledge. Besides, educated people generally are proactive in gathering information and engaging the services of advisors and other resources. It therefore is not surprising that people who turn to special institutions for help with child-rearing problems tend to be better educated.

Family Income

A family's financial situation is determined by its income and income is related to the family's size, structure and partners' ages. For example, families that are larger in size or who consist of only one parent or of a senior-aged couples tend to have lower incomes. Income obviously is lower in cases of unemployment or long-term disability. Also, average family income varies by region.

Clearly, a family can purchase more when its income is higher. A good income means that it does not have to scrimp on basic needs—it can afford various commodities such as a car or to own its own home. A family's daily routine depends on such material possessions, and their presence or absence influences child rearing. If a family is well off financially, it has advantages that benefit child rearing. A higher standard of living enables children to take courses, join clubs, take up hobbies and so forth. Money does not buy happiness, but a superior financial position creates material, social and cultural opportunities that generally benefit child rearing.

This does not mean, of course, that matters cannot go wrong in a financially well-to-do family. Prosperity does not guarantee good child rearing. The generally favorable position of the more prosperous family can turn from an advantage into a disadvantage, particularly if the child has no financial worries and is spoiled as well.

Occupation of the Father

The occupation of the father (in most cases, the main breadwinner) also puts its stamp on the family. What the occupation and professional status of the father mean for the family in financial terms has already been addressed. The relationship of his profession to other relevant factors (e.g., his educational level and background) has also been noted. What remains to be discussed is the intrinsic significance of the father's profession to the family.

The extent to which the father is occupationally satisfied influences his well-being and mood. The latter will affect family life because he will behave in a more relaxed manner at home if he enjoys his work. The family also experiences the father's profession in terms of the number of hours he has to be away for his work, the scheduling of his working hours and the amount of time he can devote to his family.

On the other hand, if the father is unemployed or on disability, this may also touch the family constellation because he spends more time at home. This extended presence may cause tensions in the family, both between the parents and between the parents and their children. Unemployment can become a frustrating affair for the unemployed. Some feel inferior and think that they have failed in their job or feel worthless because they are not able to support their family. Others feel short-changed and unfairly treated because they take second place to those who are employed. It is obvious that this will influence the family atmosphere and child rearing.

Employment of the Mother

The mother's employment also has consequences for the family and the child-rearing process. Following the Second World War, a growing number of women began working outside the home. During the first years after the war, it was mainly women from lower socio-economic groups who went out of the home to work, but in subsequent years the phenomenon became more commonplace and now involves all socio-economic levels.

The reasons women work outside the home have changed over the years. Originally, the reason was mainly economic; that is, to help support the family financially or to afford something extra (e.g., vacation, car, home or clothing). Later on, other reasons gained in importance: to escape the monotony of housekeeping and to achieve personal fulfilment.

The least that can be said for a mother's employment is that it improves the family's material circumstances. To the mother, it may mean liberation from housework. She may enjoy her job or view it as personally gratifying. All this may positively influence her sense of well-being. She will be able to function better not only in her job but also in her family and child-rearing duties. Furthermore, working outside the home affects such things as the time that the mother is absent from the home and the way in which her children are cared for when she is at work.

Generally speaking, a mother employed outside the home has less time to spend with her children than a mother who remains at home. This is especially the case when she has a time-consuming job or when the father is either absent or shirks household and child-rearing responsibilities. For the mother, this means a heavier workload and greater psychological stress, which in turn influences her behavior in ways that are not beneficial to child rearing.

Sometimes a mother has no choice but to work outside the home, particularly in low-income or single-parent families. For people in less favorable economic circumstances, the main concern is to survive financially, even if it is at the expense of child rearing.

It has been found that the traditional roles of husband and wife break down in families in which the mother works. Role differences become less defined and more egalitarian as the partners exchange some of their functions.

Social Status

Some factors affecting child-rearing practices are inherent to the family's social position. Families of higher economic status differ in their child-rearing practices from those of lower socio-economic status.

At the lower socio-economic level, child rearing centers on teaching conformity. Children are taught to adapt in various ways: first, to conform to their own milieu (within the family to the parents' ideas), but also to adjust to the demands of society's institutions, rules, regulations and laws. Deviating ideas and behaviors are not appreciated. Child rearing emphasizes appropriate behavior, obedience, orderliness and respect for authority.

At the higher socio-economic level, child rearing may be less rigid. Rather than aiming at rules, regulations and laws, it focuses on interpersonal relationships and the development of personality characteristics. The child's own ideas and aberrant behavior are more readily accepted. Rather than being taught to accept things as they are, the child is taught how to explore them. In child rearing, the emphasis is on responsibility, aspirations, self-control and tolerance.

Upper and lower socio-economic groups differ in their child-rearing practices, as is apparent, for example, in their different approaches to discipline. Parents from lower socio-economic levels rely more heavily on discipline and corporal punishment. At higher socio-economic levels, punishment may be less frequent; parents instead reason with their children and explain why certain acts are wrong. Punishment is less physical and more a question of withholding love from the child (e.g., turning away from the child in a disappointed manner or ignoring the child).

Personal Factors

Personality

Just as behavior is related to one's personality, so is the way that parents raise their children dependent on the parents' personalities. An impulsive person behaves differently from a more restrained one; a modest individual has a different way of expressing himself or herself than an arrogant one. The same applies to child rearing. Optimistic parents will use different child-rearing methods than pessimistic ones. Conscientious parents will raise their children in ways that differ from those who are more permissive. Thus, approaches to child rearing are related to the abilities, temperaments, motives, incentives, interests, aspirations, ideas, norms and values of the parents which, of course, vary from person to person.

Of particular importance is how the individual characteristics of the two parents mix. It is usually assumed that parents with contrasting personalities make a better team because they complement one another. However, it also appears that parents with similar characteristics get along better. The latter situation, of course, is more beneficial to child rearing. If the parents get along well, the family usually exhibits harmony; if there are tensions between the parents, the children will also be affected because conflicts between parents nearly always influence child rearing. Sometimes, parents try to shield their children from their marital problems, mostly without success. Sometimes parents require their children to take sides. The latter may result in a struggle for the child's favor. It usually is difficult for a child to choose between the parents. Even in those cases in which the fault lies with one particular parent, the child may have difficulty abandoning that parent.

Child rearing is not only a function of the parents' personalities but also of the child's personality. Child rearing is an interpersonal process, an interaction between parents and children. Parents will, consciously or unconsciously, take into account the specific person-alities of their child. They will respond differently to a generally cheerful child than they will to a child who is often depressed. An achievement-oriented child will be treated differently than a child who is not so directed.

Age

Young parents and older parents approach child rearing different-ly. Older people behave differently than younger people. Composure and reflection replace activity and vitality. As one grows older, one's outlook on life changes. One gains in life experience, regards differ-ent matters as important and begins to realize the relative nature of things. What is significant here is that experience in child rearing increases with time. One becomes more aware of the possibilities and limitations of the child-rearing process. Generally, parents become less strict and demanding and more tolerant and permissive as they grow older.

With respect to the age of the children, it is obvious that infants, young children and adolescents must be cared for in different ways. Young children have close ties with their parents and are dependent on them, but as they grow older they will seek their own ways, which involve a progressive loosening of parental ties. Child-rearing prac-tice changes accordingly.

Sex

The last of the personal factors to be discussed is the sex of the parents and of the children. Each parent contributes to child rearing in a way that is indicative of his or her sex. Mothers traditionally have played a more emotionally expressive role and, because of this approach, tend to be the center of emotional support within the family. Their first objective is to foster a good atmosphere and good relationships within the family. They focus on pragmatic matters important to daily life and favor responsibility and obedience. Fa-thers, on the other hand, traditionally have played a more rational, instrumental role, and as a result often give a practical focus to the family. They also are oriented toward goals outside the family and thus provide the child with "a window on the outside world." Traditionally, they have emphasized social success (in career and education), discipline and self-restraint.

The sex difference in child rearing is related to male and female roles in society. There are historically established ideas about how men and women should behave. For example, the man is supposed to be active, powerful, initiating and confident in his actions, whereas the woman is expected to be dependent, caring, gentle, sensitive, understanding and not overly aggressive. Of course, this rigid assignment of roles seems to be deteriorating. Fathers are getting more involved in housekeeping and raising their children. Mothers are, increasingly, responsible for earning the family income and have assumed part of the family's disciplinary tasks (traditionally a father's job). Admittedly, these developments are taking place more frequently in young families and among families from higher socio-economic levels. Overall, however, research on family roles indicates that, in terms of hours, taking care of the house and the family is still essentially the responsibility of the woman. The husband's and children's contributions still tend to be limited in this area, although this is changing.

Parents raise their children against this background of expectations that exists vis-à-vis the sexes. Girls generally are expected to be quiet, docile, passive and indulgent, whereas boys are required to be active and energetic and to show perseverance. Therefore, boys are raised differently than girls. In fact, this differential approach starts right from birth. For example, baby boys are more likely to be fed on demand, whereas girls are more likely to be fed at fixed intervals. Consequently, boys learn that their aggressive demands are likely to be satisfied, whereas girls learn that theirs are not—and therefore begin to react passively because they find no advantage in behaving aggressively.

Accordingly, the process of raising girls traditionally has been more emotional and aimed at the development of interpersonal skills; whereas that of boys has been more rational and oriented toward achievement and future careers. Greater demands are placed on boys in terms of education and schooling; and in this respect boys are raised more strictly than girls. However, girls face greater social control than boys. Girls grow up under relatively protected circumstances inside as well as outside the family. Parents apply rules more strictly and supervise girls more closely. They grant boys more freedom, apply less control and tolerate more aggressive behavior.

Given all this, it is not surprising that boys behave differently from girls, a difference readily observed at a very young age. For example, during early childhood, boys already display more expressions of direct aggression, such as fighting and destroying things, whereas girls exhibit more indirect forms of aggression, such as scolding and gossiping. Perhaps the role expectations have already been transformed into a fixed behavioral pattern.

Finally, there is the interaction between the sex of the parents and that of the children. Generally, parents are more tolerant and permissive toward children of the opposite sex, whereas they grant children of the same sex less freedom and subject them to higher expectations.

Family Factors

Family Size

Family size has decreased over the past decades. Foremost, this decrease has been a result of the increasing popularity of modern birth control measures, which make it rather easy to prevent pregnancies. People have learned about contraceptives and are no longer hesitant to use them, even in circles which used to regard such measures with suspicion. The reasons for limiting family size are about the same as the reasons for not having children at all. They may be ideological, financial, personal or merely a question of following a trend.

A family's size has important consequences for its children. In smaller families, the children have literally and figuratively more space; whereas in larger ones the youngsters encounter one another more often. The latter situation may have positive or negative effects because the children may help, support and learn from each other or they may get in each other's way. Furthermore, when parents cannot or will not devote themselves totally to the family, the children of large families may lack in care and attention because these benefits have to be shared with too many other children. There may be too much emphasis on rules and discipline at the cost of personal attention for the child. This disadvantage may be somewhat compensated for, in that children in large families tend to raise each other, whether or not the parents request it. This may be beneficial to the group consciousness of an individual child but may place too great a burden on the shoulders of the older siblings. Moreover, it appears that the child-rearing influence that children exercise over one another is less effective than that of their parents. Although some children act as born guardians of their siblings, they are the exception rather than the norm. Generally, brothers and sisters cannot compensate for the reduced attention that parents of larger families can devote to their children.

In addition to the trend to decrease family size, couples more and more are postponing having a family. Nowadays, women have their first child about two years later than was the case in the 1960s. Delays occur particularly among the more educated couples. One consequence of such delays is the "catching-up" phenomenon that may be observed in these circles. Women with higher levels of education who are in their thirties or older give birth more often than their less-educated counterparts, who started having children earlier in life. In some cases, it concerns "last-opportunity" mothers who delayed having children as long as possible. Sometimes it involves "regretters," who initially chose not to have a family but subsequently changed their mind.

Birth Order

Studies of birth order of children have not always led to compatible results. In the past, research into the relationship between child rearing and birth order usually involved large families. Now that family size is decreasing, the results of these studies take on a different meaning. The review presented in this section will limit itself to more recent data and circumstances that pertain to smaller families: that is, the oldest child, the second child, the youngest child and the only child.

Of all the children, the oldest child is expected most eagerly. Parents are still inexperienced and usually thoroughly prepare themselves for the arrival of their firstborn. Once the baby has arrived, it enjoys a great deal of attention. The parents are intensely involved with their child, spend a lot of time with it and stimulate it in all sorts of ways. As a result, the first-born child may feel rejected once other children who also demand attention arrive (sibling rivalry). The oldest child may experience feelings of jealousy at a primitive emotional level. Expressions of jealousy toward subsequent children are not limited to firstborns, however. To prevent such behavior in all children, it is important to prepare them well for the arrival of a new brother or sister.

Generally speaking, parents raise firstborns in a stricter manner and demand more from them, particularly with respect to achievement. When other children arrive in the family, the firstborn is sometimes expected to know more and to be able to do more than the younger ones, which is often, but not always, the case. ("But you are the oldest;" "You should know better;" or "You should have more sense.") Thus, the oldest child frequently serves as an example to the younger ones. Moreover, parents may assign special duties and responsibilities to the eldest and enlist his or her help in raising the other children.

Of course, these experiences influence the personality of the eldest child. First-born children often grow up to be persons with a great need for achievement, particularly at the intellectual level. Later on in life, they may become conservative and perhaps somewhat rigid individuals who adhere to strict rules. They are conscientious, cooperative and oriented toward others but also rather insecure and sensitive to other people's opinions. They are often not very spontaneous and adventurous.

Second children—and subsequent children—grow up with the knowledge of having a sibling above them who knows better and is more capable. They may follow the example set by the oldest child or rebel against it. Parents place fewer demands on their second and subsequent children. Thus, these children are allowed to grow up in a more relaxed manner in the shadow of an older brother or sister. Second children are generally less conscientious, less pessimistic, more easy-going, livelier and sometimes more restless.

Like the eldest, the youngest child gets quite a bit of attention, not only from the parents but also from the other children. The latter is especially the case when there is a great difference in age between the siblings. Sometimes the youngest child is spoiled. In that case, he or she may grow up to be a dependent individual who always relies on others.

Only children are simultaneously the oldest and youngest child in the family. However, they tend to be raised in a manner that resembles the treatment received by an oldest rather than a youngest child. Only children have a very intense relationship with their parents; all their lives they receive a lot of personal attention and do not have to fear competition from other children. Thus, they may develop into socially introverted, independent individuals who do not need others. However, if they are spoiled, they may grow up to become dependent individuals who always rely upon other people.

CHILD-REARING EXPERIENCES AND TRADITIONS

The experiences parents accumulate during their lives, especially during their childhood, influence the way that they raise their children. These events are related to such factors as their educational and intellectual development, the size and socio-economic level of the family in which they were raised, whether they grew up in an urban or rural setting and so forth.

Of particular importance is the child rearing they experienced themselves because this may influence the manner in which they raise their children. Usually, parents will use child-rearing methods that relate to and are a continuation of the way they were raised themselves. This "repetition through the generations" phenomenon may be referred to as a child-rearing tradition. The presence of such a tradition can be easily demonstrated by comparing the child-rearing approaches of successive generations. Thus, grandparents, great-grandparents and other ancestors may indirectly influence the way in which subsequent generations are raised.

Parents may imitate their own child rearing subconsciously or consciously. We find conscious imitation in parents who believe that they have been raised well and who want to provide their children with a similar experience. On the other hand, those who regard their own rearing as unsatisfactory often subconsciously repeat their parents' methods. For example, parents who were neglected when young may have failed to learn how to establish good relationships with their own children. Often, they will neglect their own offspring. Another remarkable example of a subconscious tradition is child abuse by parents who themselves were victims of child abuse.

Some parents make a conscious effort to raise their children in a way that is different from the manner in which they themselves were raised. In this compensational type of child rearing, parents wish to give their children what they themselves lacked. Parents who suffered a cold and harsh childhood try to create for their own children a warm family environment. Or parents who feel that they were not given enough opportunities during childhood will try to stimulate their children in as many ways as possible. But even in those cases, it is possible to find similarities between the way the parents raise their children and their own child-rearing experiences. Traditions are hard to break.

CHILD-REARING POLICY

The child-rearing policy of parents may be viewed as the practical application of their attitudes toward child rearing. By "policy" is meant the conglomeration of rules, methods and measures that parents deem necessary for their child rearing to be successful.

Intuition Versus Objectivity

Child-rearing policy entails intuitive as well as objective aspects. There are parents who raise their children almost exclusively on the basis of intuition, without too much thought about why they act the way they do. This does not necessarily mean that they just stumble along and do not comprehend what they are involved in or what the consequences of their child rearing will be. However, they do lack a clear child-rearing ideal and an articulate child-rearing plan. Their policies are primarily based on their natural child-rearing talents. Other parents, on the other hand, have a very definite policy reflecting their ideas concerning child rearing. They have a clear ideal in mind, know what they wish to achieve and have thoughts on how to realize this goal. This reflects an objective child-rearing attitude.

The child-rearing policies of most parents contain intuitive as well as objective aspects; indeed, both are necessary for successful results. Besides possessing good intuition, parents should be aware of the goals they wish to achieve and the possibilities and limitations associated with the various stages of child development.

Characteristics of Policy

Strictness

Child-rearing policies are characterized by the degree of strictness expressed in their application. In a strict policy, the parents feel that their children should know their place, and their policy is accompanied by a whole range of rules and regulations. Such strict policies are especially prevalent in intolerant child rearing. It should be clear that the developing child will not benefit very much from an overly strict child-rearing policy. It is much better if something is left to the intuition and creativity of the child.

Consistency

A critical aspect of a child-rearing policy is the consistency with which it is applied. A good policy by definition is a consistent one. It is important for children to know where they stand and what their parents expect of them. This way they will feel secure, particularly because the consistent response of the parents provides them with norms for their behavior.

An inconsistent child-rearing policy may involve parents treating their children with love and attention one time and with indifference or neglect the next—or demanding a lot at one moment and indulging too much at another. An inconsistent policy is characterized by an erratic application of child-rearing methods. Identical behavior displayed by a child is randomly approved or condemned. This makes the child insecure because if the parents approve a particular behavior one moment and reject it the next, the behavior in question will take on conflicting values for the youngster. When the behavior is approved, the child will associate it with positive feelings; when it is disapproved, the child will link it with negative ones. In the first situation, the child will try to repeat the behavior; whereas in the latter, the child will not repeat it. In other words, in the case of an inconsistent child-rearing policy, positive and negative feelings are intermixed. This makes the child insecure and, in extreme situations, neurotic.

A consistent policy does not necessarily mean that the parents apply the procedures rigidly, overly control the child or immediately intervene when a behavior falls outside the framework of their policy. If this were the case, it would be labeled as a strict child-rearing policy, which, as has been noted, is not beneficial for the child's personality development. A consistent child-rearing policy is best carried out with a certain flexibility and limited strictness. What is of importance is that children learn to understand the general design of their parents' policy and know where they stand. This will provide them with guidelines for their actions.

CHILD-REARING METHODS

Reward and Punishment

The most commonly applied methods in child rearing are reward and punishment—parents reward desired behaviors and punish undesired ones. The idea behind this approach is the expectation that children will repeat behaviors for which they are rewarded and eliminate those for which they are punished.

Psychological findings suggest that rewarding desired behaviors is much more effective than punishing undesired ones. The teaching benefits of punishment are limited. Punishment emphasizes that particular behaviors are not allowed, but it does not indicate what should be done instead. Thus, it might be advisable to punish as little as possible, particularly in situations where opportunities to reward are available. For example, if a child treats his younger siblings too roughly, it will be more effective to reward him when he is gentle with them than to punish him when he is rough. In reality, however, parents usually punish more often than they reward. The pedagogical literature's devotion of vastly more space to the question of punishment than to reward may be related to this.

In general, children are more affected by reward than by punishment. If a child is rewarded, chances are good that the child will repeat the behavior that led to the reward. The effects of punishment are less predictable and various outcomes are possible. The behavior may be completely, partially or temporarily eliminated, or it may continue and even increase in frequency. A temporary effect of punishment may be that the undesired behavior is suspended as long as the penalty is applied or threatened. In itself, this temporary effect is not necessarily negative. This may be the case, for example, if parents deem that a certain behavior is not always undesirable but only temporarily undesirable or undesirable in certain circumstances.

Some Rules

Rewards or punishments should be administered in adequate dosages. Weak responses do not leave a lasting impression on the child and thus will not have sufficient effect. On the other hand, excessive rewards and punishments immunize the child against their effectiveness.

Rewards or punishments should be given at the right time, preferably immediately following the behavior in question. It makes less sense to reward or punish a child at some later time because, in that case, the relationship between the behavior and the reward or punishment will not be apparent to the child.

Rewards or punishments should be consistent with the behavior. Thus, a child who has broken a friend's bike could be punished by having the child repair the bike or pay for the damages. This will mean more to the child than being sent to bed early, which has nothing to do with the undesired behavior.

For rewards or punishments to be optimally effective, it is necessary that the child understands their relationship to the behaviors that generated them. Particularly with respect to punishment, the parents should explain why they punish if this is not immediately clear. In cases where the child does not perceive the relationship, punishment may arouse feelings of revenge and anger, which have little positive educational value. These observations are especially important as they relate to punishment because the latter, particularly severe punishment, may have undesired side effects.

Severe Punishment

Severe punishment usually produces the opposite effect—certainly if it is perceived as unfair, if it has not been meted out at the right time or if its relationship to the undesired behavior is not apparent to the receiver. In most cases, the children only learn not to display the undesired behavior in the presence of their parents. The possibility exists that they will continue to misbehave elsewhere or seek compensation by acting out the aggression generated in them by the punishment. In rare cases, if the child is subjected to severe punishment on a continuing basis, overt resistance to the parents may disappear altogether. The child then neurotically develops into a timid, introverted individual.

Severe punishment has negative consequences of which the following are but a few:

- It is an unpleasant experience for the child (and often for the parent);

- It impedes the child's potential, and the child's frustration may lead to aggression;

- It renders the child insecure, especially if the reason for the punishment is not explained—as a result, the child may fear a parent's reaction anytime the child is uncertain whether the parent approves of the behavior;

- It may elicit undesired tensions in the child, which may lead to nervousness, withdrawal and under-achievement in school;

- It may serve as a negative example—that is, the child may imitate the parent's aggressive behavior and it is possible that the severe example set by the parent may motivate the child to act aggressively;

- It jeopardizes the parent-child relationship because it leads to an aversion toward the persons involved in the punishing situation;

- It desensitizes the child to severe punishment, which, in the long run, will render it less effective.

The effects of severe punishment are less serious if the child has a good relationship with the parents. In an emotionally cold family environment, excessive punishment may have disastrous results. Unfortunately, excessive punishments tend to be prevalent in such families. Such parents punish severely because, in essence, they are not interested in the child and want to have little to do with child rearing.

The domineering parent, on the other hand, has definite and inflexible ideas about child rearing and education, in which punishment occupies a logical position. That is, the parent will punish behaviors that do not fit his or her conformist norms.

Mild Punishment

Punishment takes place in all child rearing, although the frequency of punishment differs. Even though rewards undoubtedly have advantages over punishments, this does not mean that parents should never punish. Parents cannot tolerate everything and in some cases are forced to punish. In any case, remaining passive when a child misbehaves also may have negative consequences. The child will readily interpret this as approval of the behavior. Moreover, the undesired behavior itself often is a pleasant experience for the child and thus already has a rewarding effect.

A widespread misconception is that one can better force a child to abandon undesired behavior by using severe rather than mild punishment. In fact, the only benefit of severe punishment is that it allows parents to vent their heated temper. Some parents realize this and willingly admit that this is sometimes the reason for punishment.

Mild punishment has many advantages over severe punishment. It is more effective and has fewer of the negative side effects mentioned above. Mild punishment is not detrimental to the parent-child relationship and enables parent and child to forgive and forget more readily. There are no tensions and the parent does not make the child feel insecure and frustrated. The youngster learns to live with punishment and is able to maintain an equilibrium when punished by others (e.g., a teacher).

Mild punishment occurs mainly in warm or permissive child-rearing environments. In such environments, the good relationship that exists between parent and child results in the punishment being quite mild. In permissive child-rearing milieus, punishment may be mild or even non-existent for a number of reasons. The parents may be indifferent toward the child, incapable of punishing the child or have a conscious child-rearing philosophy that excludes punishment.

Ways of Rewarding and Punishing

The discussion thus far has focused on the quantitative aspect of reward and punishment. In the following paragraphs, we will review the various ways of rewarding and punishing as they may occur in child rearing.

Sometimes, rewards or punishments take the form of distinct, overt actions on the part of the parents. In such cases, a reward may, for instance, involve providing the child with something extra (e.g., extra allowance) and a punishment of withholding some privileges (e.g., not allowing the child to go swimming). However, reward or punishment may be more subtle. A reward may be an encouraging remark, a single gesture or a smile, whereas a punishment may simply consist of letting the child know that one does not agree with the child's actions. Here too, a gesture or a remark may be sufficient. The attitude and facial expression of the parent are often enough to indicate that a behavior is regarded as desirable or undesirable. These subtleties in the long run can exert an important influence on the personality development of the child.

One of the most effective ways of rewarding or punishing appears to be the manipulation of love. This is particularly effective when the parent-child relationship is a good one. Parents reward their children by showing a loving attitude and punish them by giving signs of disappointment. Parental acceptance (reward) and rejection (punishment) apparently make a strong impression on children. In principle, they adapt their behavior to that of their parents more out of fear of losing parental love than out of fear of more overt punishment.

Setting an Example

Neither conversing and reasoning with the child nor rewarding or punishing will have much of an effect if the parents themselves do not set a good example. Providing positive role models is an important aspect of child rearing.

Children have a tendency to imitate their parents' behavior and adopt their ideas. A long time may pass between observing the example and subsequent imitation, and thus the relationship between example and imitation may not be obvious at first. That is why parents are sometimes surprised about their children's actions and ideas, even though the latter have in fact been copied from them. It does not have to be a literal imitation; it is more the essence of the behavior and ideas of the parent that the child tries to copy. Thus, a child may imitate a parent's dishonesty in situations that are completely different from those in which the child originally observed the behavior. Or, if parents teach a child that lying is wrong but do not refrain from lying themselves in certain situations, the child will probably learn only that it is wrong to lie in certain situations. The child may come to the conclusion, however, that it is okay to lie in other situations, when it is convenient.

A child will imitate parental examples if there is a good parent-child relationship. Imitation will occur more readily in family settings and children from such families will more closely resemble their parents in behavior and attitudes. But in a cold environment (where the relationship is less good), the parents also serve as models. The children may imitate the parental example or rebel against it. Parental behavior will be an influential factor, whatever the child-rearing style.

5
CHILD REARING AND PERSONALITY DEVELOPMENT

CHILD REARING

Basic Concepts

Child rearing is a complicated process with many interacting forces and influences, including the personality of the child and the personality of the parents and their ideas about child rearing. Parents vary in their views about what should and should not be done when raising children. Within the family, elders may disagree with one another about which approach should be taken. Furthermore, it is possible that parental attitudes toward one child differ from those toward another. Consequently, it is not easy for a person who studies child rearing to gain a clear understanding of the overall process.

In investigating parental child-rearing practices and their effects on children, two basic approaches are possible. One may take the *molecular approach*, in which one selects a particular area of child rearing (e.g., toilet training, sexual development) and attempts to isolate patterns specific to that area of interest; or one may opt for the *molar approach,* in which one focuses on patterns underlying the overall child-rearing process.

This book takes the latter approach. We assume that the whole of child rearing influences the personality development of the child and focus attention on two concepts applicable to the child rearing

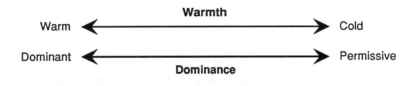

Figure 1
Dimensions of Child Rearing

atmosphere and all its practices and methods—namely, parental *warmth* and *dominance*.

The concepts of warmth and dominance appear in many popular and professional publications about child rearing, although not always in the same explicit manner and often under different names. The two concepts are found in studies conducted in various countries and cultures and appear to have international validity. They may appropriately be called *basic concepts* of child rearing.

Warmth in child rearing is defined as the "horizontal distance between parent and child," by which is meant the emotional distance or the degree to which the parent-child relationship is characterized by warmth and love or by coldness and rejection. *Dominance in child rearing* refers to the "vertical distance between parent and child," or the extent to which the parent dominates and controls the child or allows freedom and autonomy.

Both concepts involve dimensions with poles reflecting extreme and opposing child-rearing practices. On the basis of their child-rearing patterns, parents can be placed somewhere within these dimensions. Some parents are very warm, others cold, and many somewhere in between. The same applies to the level of dominance they exercise.

The remainder of this chapter is concerned with these two concepts. They are presented as separate dimensions and the discussion is limited to the polar extremes.

The Warm-Cold Dimension in Child Rearing

The most important aspect of child rearing is probably the extent to which the relationship between parents and child is characterized by warmth and emotional closeness. This general aspect reflects the overall ambience within families and consequently permeates all facets of child rearing.

Warm Child Rearing

In *warm child rearing*—which will be presented here in its ideal form—parents and children have good personal contact. The parents accept their children as they are, with all their shortcomings and failures. As a result, the children feel safe and protected. They trust their parents and know that the latter will support them and help them when they encounter difficulties or problems. The trust is mutual; the two parties confide in each other and openly express affection for one another. Warm parents are emotionally involved in the activities of their children. They provide a lot of care and attention, stimulate their youngsters in many ways and are available when needed. Intellectually, the children receive help with homework and are praised when they do well in school. Socially, they are encouraged to make contacts and bring home friends. There is also much involvement in other areas—parents, for example, spend a great deal of time with their children on weekends, play with them, take them on outings and so forth.

When warm parents punish their children, they do so in moderation and with good reason. Rewards play an important role in their child rearing and they discuss unacceptable behaviors with their children. Physical punishment is an exception rather than the rule. Warm parents prefer to show love when their children have done something right and disappointment when they have done something wrong.

Warm child rearing is particularly found in harmonious families, where there are few tensions and conflicts. It usually involves balanced families, where the members have a strong sense of belonging, get along well, show a great deal of affection and love and do many things together.

The basis for this good relationship is that the parents get along well. They perform their parental tasks to the best of their abilities and do their utmost to ensure that the family runs smoothly.

Cold Child Rearing

Cold child rearing is in every sense the opposite of warm child rearing. The attitude of cold parents toward their children is superficial, indifferent, negative, rejecting and in some cases even hostile. The parents do not accept their children, a large emotional distance exists between them and they withhold understanding and support. They ignore their children and give them little stimulation. The parents devote little time and effort to their youngsters, often regard them as a nuisance and may neglect them.

Cold parents do not enjoy the parental role, and they may try to shirk parental and domestic duties. They have an egotistical attitude and go their own way without consulting other family members.

Cold parents punish a lot, often resorting to physical measures. Discipline is arbitrary. They rely more on disapproval than approval and often use fear or threats as a child-rearing practice.

Cold child rearing is primarily found in disharmonious families, in which the internal relationships are problematic. Family members do not get along very well and basically do not care about each other. Parents often disagree about the manner in which their children should be raised. They criticize each other; for example, the husband may feel that his wife dominates the family, whereas the latter may maintain that her husband does not live up to his responsibilities.

The Dominance-Permissiveness Dimension in Child Rearing

Dominance refers to the extent to which parents try to control their children and push them in a particular direction without leaving them much room for self-actualization. The concept, unlike warmth, is not a homogenous one. It may include several different aspects, including overt or covert dominance of the child, the presence of family rules and a parent's demanding attitude.

Dominant Child Rearing

Dominant parents demonstrate a need to possess their children. They concern themselves with virtually everything their children do, and they want to control all their actions. Dominant parents try to force their point of view on their children. They are very demanding, set all kinds of limitations and often make strong suggestions which they expect the children to follow. Basically, dominant parents attempt to force their child in a direction they want the child to go without paying sufficient attention to the youngster's individuality. As a result, the child is to a large extent dependent on the parents. The child's expressions are inhibited and opportunities to develop independent activities are limited. Dominant child rearing often means that the parents help their children with virtually everything, including homework, hobbies and career choice (sometimes too much so, in the child's opinion). The parents also keep a close eye on the children's health and general development.

Dominant child rearing often includes a complete framework of rules (e.g., house rules concerning tidiness, neatness, modesty, table manners and curfew) that are rigidly enforced. The parents are rather demanding and expect quite a few achievements. They feel that their children should be active and they abhor daydreaming and idleness. They try to accelerate the development of their children in many ways. They expect their youngsters to get good marks in school and to be achievement-oriented in other areas.

Domineering parents demand absolute obedience and do not tolerate opposition; disobedience is met with anger. They often act in an authoritarian manner, use a lot of pressure and are tough in their child-rearing practices. They very much believe in strong discipline and rely heavily on (physical) punishment.

Dominant child rearing is usually found in closed families with little contact with the external world, where the parents occupy a central position. The father is the head of the family and the one who maintains discipline. The mother focuses on domestic matters and as a result has little chance to develop herself in other areas. The closed character of the family means that the children grow up in social isolation. Yet they learn to conform to what the community expects and to closely adhere to society's rules and regulations.

Permissive Child Rearing

Permissive child rearing is the opposite of dominant child rearing. Permissive parents do not force themselves upon their children, but in fact leave them a great deal of freedom. They exert no pressure and take little or no corrective action when the children do something wrong. Permissive parents demand very little of their children and do not expect great achievements (e.g., in school). The children can be involved in useless activities or just remain idle, without the parents doing anything about it. The family has few rules and does not strictly enforce the few that do exist. If the family does resort to punishment, it is inconsistent.

Because permissive parents do not demand much and do not stimulate their children, the latter may grow up to become good-for-nothings. If this "laissez faire" approach is paired with a warm attitude, the children may be spoiled. When combined with a cold attitude, the child rearing may be distant and indifferent.

Permissive child rearing is primarily found in families that have few strong ties. Social contacts are predominately sought outside the family, with neighbors and friends.

Interaction Between the Two Dimensions

Careful observation of relationships between parents and children reveals that parent-child interaction is not a simple, one-dimensional process. The relationship between elders and their offspring does not simply consist of variation along a single dimension but rather is characterized by an interaction between the parents' two child-rearing attitudes. Thus, children may grow up in an environment that is warm and domineering, warm and permissive, cold and domineering or cold and permissive. Any combination and gradation is possible. Furthermore, generalizations can be made about the relationship between parent-child interaction and personality development of children when the interplay between the two dimensions is taken into consideration.

Previously, we referred to the warmth dimension as the horizontal distance between parent and child and the dominance dimension as the vertical distance between parent and child. These descriptions

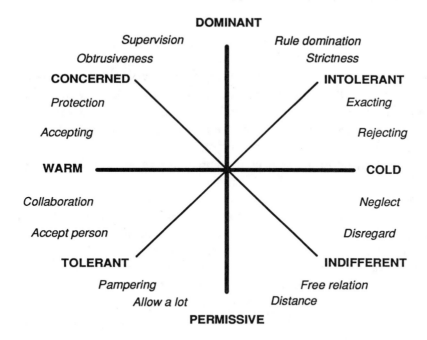

Figure 2
A Circular Model of Child Rearing

already indicate how the two basic concepts may be combined into a model of child rearing. They form the primary axes of the model presented in Figure 2.

Besides the two main dimensions, the model has two secondary axes, which may be regarded as combinations of the primary ones. The *tolerance-intolerance* axis represents *democracy* in child rearing and differentiates between parents who are warm and permissive and those who are domineering and cold. The *concerned-indifferent* axis refers to the degree of parental *involvement* in child rearing and contrasts a warm and domineering attitude with a cold and permissive one. These axes of the model form the dimensions in which every kind of child rearing can be placed.

The Role of Warmth and Dominance in Child Rearing

The discussion thus far has focused on the concepts of warmth and dominance in their general sense. It was noted that these concepts may be found at the core of the various types of child rearing. In other words, the concepts of warmth and dominance have a certain degree of consistency and general applicability. In everyday child rearing, however, warmth and dominance are not necessarily of equal importance and do not always appear in the same form. In each specific child-rearing situation, they have a different, unique character that is adapted to the circumstances.

Warmth and dominance also play different parts in the child-rearing behavior of *fathers* and *mothers* and in the raising of *boys* and *girls*. These differences are related to the traditional division of roles between the sexes in our society—children tend to regard the father in terms of dominance and the mother in terms of warmth.

Notwithstanding the fact that many exceptions to the rule exist, maternal warmth is generally more emotional in nature than paternal warmth. Mothers have an emotional involvement (positive or negative) with the child and an overt expression (or lack) of affection. Warm mothers relate intensively in a friendly, protective way with their children, whereas cold mothers reject and eventually treat their children with hostility.

Paternal warmth is less emotional in character than maternal warmth. It primarily reflects the extent to which the father accepts the child and the extent to which he establishes and maintains contact. Compared to mothers, paternal coldness expresses itself in neglect of the children, not wishing to be responsible for them and not caring about them. While cold mothers may communicate negatively, cold fathers may evade communication altogether.

Maternal dominance expresses itself mainly as protectiveness and the suppression of undesired behaviors, such as expressions of aggression. Paternal dominance is foremost reflected in a father seeking to control the child, demanding obedience and exercising strict discipline.

Maternal warmth for a son is characterized by affection, whereas paternal warmth for a son is shown by the father's acceptance of his son. For girls the opposite is true—maternal warmth is reflected in the mother's acceptance of her daughter and paternal warmth by the father's affection.

Mothers show their dominance toward their sons by protective and concerned attitudes, whereas fathers show their dominance toward their sons in intrusive behavior. With daughters, maternal dominance shows itself as protectiveness and paternal dominance as a strict disciplinary attitude.

Changing Roles

In a previous chapter, we noted that, as a result of changes in sex-role assignments, the parents' roles in child rearing are becoming increasingly similar. Thus, warmth is becoming more prominent in paternal child rearing and dominance in maternal child rearing.

The qualitative differences between the warmth and the dominance of fathers and mothers are also diminishing. Finally, as noted previously, differences in the ways that boys and girls are raised are decreasing. These recent trends should be kept in mind when analyzing child-rearing practices today.

PERSONALITY

Behavior, Personality and Situation

Variation in parental warmth and dominance creates different child-rearing environments. If the quality of the encounters between parents and children exerts a influence on the development of the children, then it is understandable that this will influence the personality development of those affected.

The philosopher Leibniz once said that, in the whole world, no two leaves are identical. The same is true of human beings—everybody is unique with his own, individual personality. Nevertheless, it is also true that people resemble one another with respect to certain aspects of their personality. These people have comparable personality characteristics and similar personality types. They also display a certain similarity in their behavior in various situations.

Behavior is not only influenced by personality but also by the environment in which it takes place. If one compares the behavior of the same person in different situations, one will most likely notice differences. One may even get the impression that one is dealing with a different person. In reality, it is only a question of different situations because human beings behave differently in different situations.

When asked how they perceive their own personality, most people will answer that they feel that they possess a relatively stable identity; that is, a personality with consistent characteristics, which they carry from situation to situation. However, in the eyes of others in their environment, they appear to possess as many personalities as there are situations. In fact, a person plays a different role in each situation, and, depending on the situation, others may perceive him or her as a different individual.

There is a continuous interaction between personality and situation that results in actual behavior. Personality characteristics should not be viewed as static entities that reside somewhere in the person and inevitably lead to particular behaviors—situational factors also play a role. Thus, a *personality characteristic* may be defined as a behavioral disposition that indicates the possibility and probability that a certain behavior will manifest itself in a certain situation.

On the other hand, situations, in as much as they influence behavior, are not independent of the person. Even though behavior reflects the situation, it is also influenced by the individual's personality. The situation can only be expressed in behavior through the personality; that is to say, through the subjective interpretation given by the person to the situation.

To what extent behavior is caused by the personality or by the situation? This varies from person to person, from personality characteristic to personality characteristic and from situation to situation. Sometimes, a person or personality characteristic will be more dominant in one situation than in another. At other times, the situation will have more influence on one person or personality characteristic than on another. In other words, some people or personality characteristics are more situation-related than others. Behavior in a situation that leaves few possibilities for personal expression will be less influenced by personality characteristics than would that same behavior in a situation where the personality could freely express itself.

The behavior of some people is primarily influenced by internal factors (personality characteristics), whereas others are primarily motivated by external considerations (situations). The former group have their own opinions and contribution to make; relatively speaking, their behavior is pretty consistent over different situations. The latter group involves individuals who are more "situation-sensitive" and generally adjust their behavior to the circumstances and reactions of other people—their behavior varies from one situation to another.

Basic Concepts

In the discussion of child rearing, we distinguished two basic concepts. Such a reduction is also possible with respect to personality, in which the basic concepts are *extroversion* and *emotionality* (emotional instability, neuroticism). In what follows we will present the two concepts as dimensions (*extroversion-introversion* and *emotionality-stability*) and discuss their extremes (which may be viewed as opposing personality types).

Extroversion

Extroverted people are oriented toward the world around them. They are spontaneous, lively, have an answer to everything and generally do not worry too much. Extroverts are sociable; they love contact with others and usually have many acquaintances. They need company because they have trouble entertaining themselves. When left alone, they may even get into trouble.

Extroverts are talkative and cheerful; they enjoy jokes and good stories. Sometimes they are impulsive and act on the spur of the moment. They like change and diversion. On occasion, they can be restless and unable to control their feelings.

Introversion

Introverts are the opposite of extroverts. They are more inwardly directed, have little need for expression and are self-contained. They are reserved and do not need to have many people around them, except for a few good friends. In groups, they tend to remain in the background.

Introverts are quiet and aloof. They like orderliness, serenity and comfort. They are independent, have their own opinions and go their own way. They are patient and earnest, reflect on things and tend to take matters rather seriously. Furthermore, they are rational, distrust impulsive actions and usually control their feelings.

Emotionality

Emotional people are characterized by a mood that can swing up and down without apparent reason. They are vulnerable, easily upset and worry a lot. As a result, they may suffer from depression and may need others to cheer them up. They tend to exaggerate and often worry about things that are really not that important, which sometimes causes them to suffer from insomnia. In their depression, they may suffer from feelings of inferiority, guilt and self-pity. They are sensitive and do not easily accept criticism. Sometimes, they suffer from physical complaints and fatigue due to psychological causes. They often have trouble concentrating and sometimes feel overwhelmed by things.

Stability

Stable people are not very vulnerable and not easily thrown off course. They see matters in their proper perspective and do not take things personally. They don't worry about trivialities and know how to differentiate between what is important and what is not. They do not have more problems than is necessary and do not exaggerate minor matters. Their mood is stable; if it fluctuates, there is usually a clear reason.

As was the case with the child-rearing dimensions, very few people represent the extremes of the personality dimensions—most fall somewhere in the middle. There are few extreme extroverts, just as there are few pure introverts. The same applies to extremely emotional and extremely stable persons. Most people are somewhat extroverted, introverted, emotional and stable.

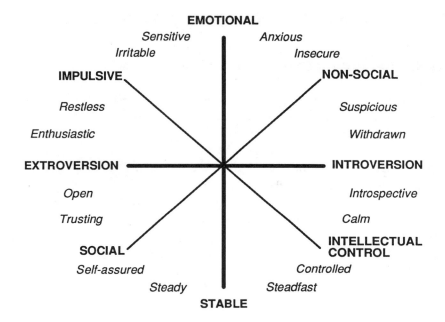

Figure 3
A Dimensional-Circular Model of Personality

A Dimensional-Circular Personality Model

Starting with the above described dimensions of personality, it is possible to create a personality model in which these dimensions form the primary axes (Figure 3). The horizontal axis represents the extroversion-introversion dimension, and the vertical axis depicts the emotionality-stability polarity. Further included are two secondary axes, namely, *impulsiveness* versus *intellectual control*, and *social* versus *non-social*.

CHILD REARING AND PERSONALITY

A Child-Rearing Personality Model

Many authors, representing varying theoretical positions, have suggested a causal relationship between child rearing and the personality development of children. This notion appears in the psychoanalytical literature, in publications based on learning theory and in papers written by anthropologically oriented authors. Often, the proponents stress the relationship between child rearing and the development of specific personality characteristics, such as aggression, conformity, ambition and so forth.

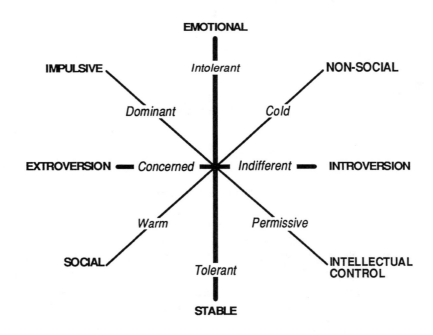

Figure 4
A Child-Rearing Personality Model

Thus far, this chapter has presented two separate models—namely, one pertaining to child rearing and one pertaining to personality. To what extent are these two models related? In other words, which child-rearing approaches result in which personality characteristics?

The child rearing and personality models may be combined into a third one, which comprises the various basic concepts as discussed in this chapter (Figure 4). The following sections discuss this relationship between child rearing and personality in more detail.

Practical Child Rearing

The main purpose of child rearing is, or should be, to provide children with an opportunity to grow up and develop in a harmonious and happy way. But people have different ideas about what is meant by child rearing and particularly about what should be the goal of this process. Some parents want their children to grow into well-adjusted adults who conform to the rules; others think it is more important that their youngsters develop a unique personality and therefore do not emphasize conformity as much. Some parents stress achievement, while others regard this as insignificant. There are many such differences and these explain why child-rearing methods may vary.

The particular form that child rearing takes will have consequences for the child's personality development. The remainder of this chapter is concerned with observations of a more pragmatic nature. We will review the possible practical consequences of eight forms of child rearing.

The two basic child-rearing dimensions of warmth and dominance form the basis for the first four child-rearing approaches: namely, *warm, cold, dominant* and *permissive* child rearing. The two secondary dimensions of democracy and involvement give rise to four additional approaches: *tolerant* or *democratic* child rearing (also called *anti-authoritarian*), *intolerant* or *authoritarian* child rearing, *concerned* child rearing, and *indifferent* child rearing. The latter four represent combinations of the four basic categories, and because of this, our discussion of these will be unavoidably repetitious at times. To avoid this as much as possible, we will keep the respective descriptions as succinct as possible. Where applicable, we will refer to the four basic forms of child rearing.

Warm Versus Cold Child Rearing

Warm Child Rearing

Warm child rearing refers to a family atmosphere in which the parents (and the other family members) accept the child. As a result, the latter feels safe and comfortable and develops a basic sense of security and belonging. Such circumstances are quite conducive to positive personality development. The parents may even make relatively large mistakes in their child rearing without experiencing dire consequences. Because of the good relationship that exists, the child can accept and adjust to the mistakes and shortcomings of the parents.

Children in warm families have every opportunity to grow up harmoniously and consequently tend to develop positive personality characteristics. Because their parents accept them as individuals, they come to realize that they are human beings with an unique personality and identity. It is very important for them to see themselves as independent individuals and to accept themselves with all their weaknesses and shortcomings. They will view themselves as worthwhile and will not likely suffer from inferiority and guilt feelings. Because warmly raised children feel safe and know they can depend on their parents, they seldom suffer from insecurity and fear.

Generally speaking, these children grow up to be independent people with a personal point of view. They are enterprising, achievement-oriented and not easily discouraged. They tend to be stable, extroverted, self-assured and self-controlled individuals with an optimistic outlook on life. Their behavior is characterized by flexibility and spontaneity. They generally feel secure in new and strange situations and know how to manage themselves. They know the rules of life, are socially well adapted and do not create tensions. Insecurity only appears when they are treated coldly, an attitude they do not know how to handle.

In exceptional instances, warm child rearing may also have negative consequences for the personality development of the child. This is particularly the case when extremely warm child rearing is combined with unfavorable circumstances, such as an indulgent and spoiling parental attitude.

Cold Child Rearing

Children raised in a cold manner may at an early age display behavioral problems (e.g., feeding problems, bed wetting and expressions of aggression). Such children develop into introverted people who are socially withdrawn and not very interested in others. They have received so little personal attention from their parents that they have never learned to care for others and do not really know how to communicate socially. The poor relationship with their parents often has left them with a limited ability to empathize with others and establish social contacts.

Children from cold family environments often have identity problems, suffer low self-esteem and feel insecure. They believe that life is largely determined by factors over which they have no control. If the child rearing is extremely cold, they may become unstable people who live under a great deal of tension and suffer neurotic symptoms. They are often dissatisfied, suspicious and hostile, which in turn may lead to rebellion, craving for attention, aggression, and anti-social and delinquent behavior.

The parents' poor, impersonal relationship and limited interest in the children forces the children to fend for themselves from an early age. As a result, they develop a certain degree of superficial independence, but this independence is usually more imaginary than real. Real independence is more often found in children from a warm family background. For children from a cold environment, it is more a question of making the best of what they have. Under the mask of independence is often hidden a large amount of dependence and need for support.

Dominant Versus Permissive Child Rearing

Dominant Child Rearing

Child rearing is not so much a question of "making the child grow up" as it is a matter of "allowing the child to grow up." Children need a certain degree of freedom and opportunity to experiment. Dominant parents may not understand this. On the contrary, they continuously supervise their children, so that they grow up in a kind of straitjacket.

Dominantly raised youngsters often are extroverted and impulsive individuals who stick to a fixed view of life. They develop a rigid lifestyle to which they strictly adhere. They closely follow the general rules and regulations and adapt themselves to the existing norms and morals. Their life is often a routine. They do not like to make waves and prefer to avoid conflicts. They do not possess much in the way of originality, creativity or initiative. They have trouble accepting that some people have different points of view, and they often are prejudiced and intolerant.

Children who grow up under the pressures of an extremely dominant child-rearing regime do not learn to develop themselves and be independent. Even as adults, they will have trouble finding their own way and sometimes may be confronted with circumstances with which they cannot cope. They lack the support from above and obviously have not learned to improvise in situations in which parental guidance falls short. In very extreme cases, the ties to the dominant parents never or only gradually disappear.

When they are a little older, it often happens that these children escape the limitation of their extremely dominant child rearing and distance themselves from the conforming, conservative ideal that was always held up to them. When they decide to free themselves from the dominant oppression and stand on their own two feet, different problems may arise. People raised in a dominant environment have learned to live according to fixed, strict rules. They have not been taught to go their own way, to adapt to the new and the unexpected, to apply rules in a flexible way or to create new rules. Once they break with their background, they live in a vacuum. Eventually they will turn into people who (sometimes only temporarily) approach life in a detached way, are against all rules and regulations and have little direction in their lives.

Permissive Child Rearing

As has been discussed, permissive parents demand little of their children and allow them a great deal of freedom. If the permissiveness is within reason, then the consequences for the children's personality development are generally favorable. Permissively raised children become stable, introverted people who are independent and rational and know how to control their behavior intellectually. They are flexible, socially well adjusted, creative and show initiative.

Children who are raised too permissively may sometimes create problems. They grow up into selfish people with little concern for others. They do not achieve very much because little was expected or demanded from them. They are often superficial, lazy and sloppy.

Permissive child rearing may be the result of a parent's inability to control a child. These parents may have given up hope and leave it all to the child. It may also be based on a conscious child-rearing philosophy, in which the parents think it is good for the child to have a lot of freedom.

Democracy in Child Rearing

Tolerant or Democratic Child Rearing

Tolerant or *democratic child rearing* is characterized by warmth as well as permissiveness. Tolerant, democratic parents accept their children as they are, have good relationships with them and treat them in a democratic manner.

The parents consider their children as their equals. They are friendly and considerate of the wishes and desires of their youngsters. They share with them what is happening within the family. They consult them concerning family matters and encourage them to voice their opinions and not hide their criticisms. In many situations, the children may make their own decisions and thus assume responsibilities. The parents reason with their children and explain their child-rearing practices.

Democratically raised children share some of the characteristics of children brought up in a warm manner and some of those raised permissively. They grow up to be stable people with a healthy dose of self-esteem. They are self-controlled, consistent and persevering. They know what they want and express their opinions openly and freely. They know how to interact with other people in an easy and open manner and how to adjust to various situations.

In cases of uncontrolled, extreme tolerance, the children will be spoiled. In these instances, the youngsters develop into dependent and often egocentric and stubborn persons who want to be the center of attention all the time.

Democratic child rearing is often based on an objective, somewhat intellectual attitude toward child rearing. The parents have a conscious child-rearing plan that reflects their philosophy. This is, for example, the case in *anti-authoritarian child rearing*, an approach that came into existence as a reaction to the intolerant, authoritarian child rearing that previously was so prevalent in society. Young parents wanted to make a radical break and not exercise any authority in any way or form. This laudable effort, however, sometimes has resulted in disastrous consequences because parents were too permissive. The children ended up in a void without any guiding principles. The result was maladjusted children, who were difficult for themselves as well as for society.

Intolerant or Authoritarian Child Rearing

Intolerant or *authoritarian child rearing* is a cold, dominant form of child rearing. Intolerant parents demand and expect a lot from their children in many ways. They treat harshly those children who cannot or will not meet their demands. They tolerate no opposition and frown on disobedience or rebellion. The child does not have much power. This kind of child rearing is characterized by strict discipline, in which physical punishment plays a large role. The relationship between strict parents and their children is far from ideal; there is a large psychological distance with little sincere contact. Parents and children each live in their own worlds because the parents deny their children entrance to theirs.

The consequences of intolerant child rearing for the personality development of the child partially resemble those of dominant child rearing and those of cold child rearing. Children raised in this manner become passive individuals with little initiative. They are insecure and conservative people who rigidly adhere to conventions and customs. They reject deviations from the norm and seldom question authority. They are often intolerant toward others, especially others with different opinions. People who have been raised in an intolerant manner tend to be pessimistic in their outlook on life. They are vengeful and suppress a lot of things, which sometimes causes them to react impulsively and aggressively.

Involvement in Child Rearing

Concerned Child Rearing

Concerned child rearing is characterized by both warmth and dominance. Thus, it resembles warm and dominant child rearing. Concerned parents are involved with their children and interested in their activities. They have good relationships with their youngsters and want to protect them against making mistakes, even if this means that they have to sacrifice the autonomy of their children.

Children raised in a concerned environment often develop into extroverted, well-adjusted people. They may be somewhat inconsiderate and carefree and express their need for assertiveness in a somewhat egotistic manner. In cases of extreme involvement, the parents are overly anxious for their children and literally interfere with everything that concerns them. Because there is a strong emotional bond between parents and children, there is not much room left for others. The exclusiveness of this child-rearing environment inhibits personality development because the children hardly have the chance to look around and spread their wings. Such a suffocating environment creates rigid children and adults who are not flexible. They lack self-esteem and perseverance, and they are more often dependent and passive.

Indifferent Child Rearing

Indifferent child rearing is a cold, permissive child rearing. The permissiveness of indifferent parents is not based on trust, as in the case with tolerant child rearing, but more on a lack of interest. The children are in fact neglected and rejected.

It may be said that children raised in an indifferent environment have received hardly any child rearing at all. They grow up with lots of freedom, are not restricted by rules but are not attached to people either. Therefore, they have trouble forming deeper contacts with others and find it difficult to adhere to rules and regulations. They are introverted individuals who live a somewhat superficial life and exert a certain degree of rational control over their behavior.

6
CHILD REARING AND DEVIANT BEHAVIOR

DEVIANT BEHAVIOR

Deviant Behavior: The General Background

One goal of child rearing is to ensure that children behave in a socially adjusted manner. Unfortunately, this goal is not always reached, as is illustrated by the deviant behavior displayed by some children.

The term *deviant behavior* refers to conduct that society regards as unacceptable in terms of conventional norms and customs. Others consider the behavior, at the least, as bothersome and irritating. It may provoke responses from the child's family and also from authorities and social agencies. More serious forms of deviant behavior include aggressive acts, juvenile delinquency, running away from home, alcoholism and other types of drug abuse, gambling, truancy and prostitution. Less serious forms include early smoking and sexual conduct, knavery, hooliganism, insolence and impertinence.

Children who display one type of deviant behavior often exhibit one or more of the other forms as well. To a certain extent, this is the result of direct causal relationships among the various types of deviancy, with one behavior leading to another. For example, children become involved in delinquency more often during a runaway period than when they are at home; on the other hand, delinquency may cause a child to be unmanageable at home and prompt the child's decision to run away. However, this coincidence of the various forms of deviancy is primarily the result of their sharing the same *general background factors*, many of which originate in the family and in child rearing. The existence of such factors can be simply demonstrated by examining the many publications that discuss causes of specific forms of deviant behavior; such a comparison will reveal large similarities in background factors. Authors who focus their attention on only one form of deviant behavior often are unaware of this coincidence.

This common source does not mean that all forms of deviancy emphasize the same specific factors to the same extent. For example, a poor relationship with the parents is usually of greater importance in running-away behavior than in juvenile delinquency, although parent-child relationships may play a role in both forms of deviancy. Furthermore, specific, unique causes also play a role in addition to those factors common to every form of deviant behavior.

The Family

Because the family plays such an important role in the child's personality development, negative consequences are virtually predictable when less-than-optimal family conditions prevail. Deviant behavior is a case in point. Relevant investigations frequently report that adverse family circumstances contribute to the cause and maintenance of deviancy. In fact, the younger the child displaying the deviant behavior, the greater the need to look for causes within the family.

If one family member exhibits deviant behavior, chances are that other members also behave in aberrant ways. Thus, in some families, deviant behavior occurs with a striking frequency. In some families, such behavior more or less becomes a tradition transferred from one generation to another. The cause for this may very likely be found in a family's specific approach to child rearing.

The question remains as to what kind of families produce deviant children. We will discuss the most important characteristics of these families in the remainder of this chapter.

Family Size

Deviant behavior is influenced by family size in a modest but noticeable way. From a mathematical point of view, it is clear that the distribution of financial resources tends to be rather restricted in large families. This applies not only to material matters, such as clothing and food, but also, for instance, to club memberships, hobbies and the kind and level of schooling that can be afforded. The resulting frustrations may provoke a search for compensation, perhaps in the form of deviant behavior. This could mean that, particularly at the lower socio-economic level, family size and deviant behavior are associated. However, opinions on this question are divided; some researchers believe it to be the case, whereas others have found no difference between socio-economic levels.

Children in large families generally enjoy less physical living space. They have to share this already limited space with many family members, and chances are greater that they will get into each other's way. The inevitably heightened activity level in such families produces a relatively high level of stimulation. Exposure to such stimulation over a number of years may result in an increase in tolerance. As a result, children from large families may become impulsive individuals with a higher than normal need for stimulation, which they may seek to satisfy by engaging in deviant behavior.

In large families, children must share parental attention with other siblings. Parents can devote less individual time to their children, and the latter become rivals for their parents' attention. They experience fewer expressions of parental affection and less stimulation. The parents provide less supervision and raise the children in a relatively restrictive manner. Studies have found that such child-rearing characteristics are associated with deviant behavior.

Children from large families are frequently labeled in a negative manner. Society and its agencies more readily regard large families as troubled. In problem cases—particularly those involving girls—intervention is more rapid because it is assumed that large families are less capable of solving their problems.

Limited financial resources, restricted physical space, shared attention and labeling result in larger families having a lower socializing ability than smaller ones. Compared to children from small families, those from larger ones encounter greater difficulties in internalizing norms, forming an identity and developing a positive self-image. This makes them more vulnerable to deviant behavior.

Birth Order

First-born children display deviant behavior less often than their middle- and, to a lesser extent, last-born siblings. There are several reasons for this phenomenon, some of which have been mentioned in previous chapters.

First, because there are no siblings to distract the parents, firstborns receive greater attention and supervision and are brought up in a more consistent manner. Furthermore, many parents enlist the help of the oldest child in raising the children that follow; sometimes firstborns choose this role for themselves. Consequently, oldest children develop a sense of responsibility and concern for others very early in life. Firstborns often serve as models for their younger siblings. To set credible examples, they must orient themselves to the conventional adult world, something girls seem to do with greater ease than boys. Thus, firstborns generally become conscientious individuals, who by their own preference behave in an adjusted manner.

Middle children exhibit deviant behavior more often than firstborns, notwithstanding that they have the benefit of their older sibling's example. By observing the firstborn, later-born children learn how to behave and discover which behaviors are successful and which are not. The example the eldest sets will certainly have an effect but may be overshadowed by the younger children's desire to develop their own identity and be noted in the family. They may resist conforming and may reject the firstborn's lifestyle.

The youngest children, as is the case with firstborns, receive a great deal of attention, not only from their parents but also from their older brothers and sisters. However, they are raised in a much less-rigid manner than firstborns. The child rearing they receive falls somewhere between that experienced by the oldest child and that encountered by the middle children. The same phenomenon applies to the extent to which they display deviant behavior.

Finally, only children, by definition, are both the oldest and youngest child. They grow up in small families. Very few are involved in deviant behavior.

Birth order and experienced family size seem to interact. Oldest and youngest children, in relative terms, grow up in small families. The oldest child is already much more mature or has left home when the youngest one is still growing up. Because of this age spread, the contacts that oldest and youngest children have with their siblings during their developmental years tend to be restricted to those of approximately the same age. This effectively reduces the size of their family. Middle children, on the other hand, are raised in relatively larger families because of the presence of both older and younger siblings. Thus, the greater incidence of deviant behavior by middle-borns may be the result of factors associated with family size that were previously discussed.

An inverse relationship exists between the spacing of births and deviant behavior; that is, the shorter the intervals between births, the greater the chance that the children will become involved in deviant activities. Children born at close intervals grow up in a relatively large family, with all the above-mentioned limitations.

Incomplete Families

Incomplete families are families in which only one of the parents, most often the mother, is present. This may be the result of voluntary single parenthood, death of one parent, or separation or divorce.

That a family is not physically complete does not necessarily imply that it cannot function properly; it is psychological rather than physical completeness that matters. Nevertheless, the effect of family incompleteness on children is often not encouraging with respect to deviant behavior. Incomplete families tend to be materially disadvantaged because of limited income, and single parents often are preoccupied with daily survival. Consequently, their children may receive less attention and guidance. In addition, the children may lack a person with whom they can identify, and supervision may be less adequate. These children may spend more time in the streets, where their chances of being exposed to deviant behavior are greater.

The relationship between the three family structures (i.e., voluntary single parenthood, death and divorce) and the deviant behavior of children varies with each type. Families that are incomplete because of the death of a parent differ little from intact families in terms of deviant behavior. Not much is known about the relationship in voluntary single-parent families. Divorce, however, is generally regarded as a reliable predictor of deviant behavior in children.

The relationship between family incompleteness and deviancy varies with age and gender. The younger the child is when the family becomes a single-parent family, the more serious the consequences. Because family life is more important to girls, their deviant behavior is more closely related to family circumstances. Consequently, the association between family status and deviancy is more pronounced among girls. With respect to boys, it has been found that it makes a difference which parent is absent. When the father is absent, boys may lack a role model who could teach them how to come to terms with their masculinity, and this may lead to role insecurity. These youngsters may be inclined to demonstrate their masculinity through deviant behavior.

The incomplete family can be made complete again if the single parent finds a partner. Problems may develop, however, if the children do not welcome this new companion into the family; greater interpersonal distance and alienation may result. Families with a biological mother and a stepfather appear to be particularly vulnerable, as is suggested by the deviant behavior frequently found among children from such a background.

The relationship between family completeness and deviant behavior may be explained in part by a labeling process. People in the neighborhood and officials from agencies (e.g., school, police and justice system) tend to regard children from incomplete families differently than they view those from "normal" families. These professionals take measures (e.g., removing children from the home or bringing them to the attention of the police) more readily when children from incomplete families are involved, particularly when the situation concerns girls.

Family Relationships

Children who display deviant behavior often come from disharmonious families lacking adequate interpersonal relationships. In such families, children are unable to find direction and may be confused. This makes identification difficult and leads to alienation, avoidance and escape behavior.

The atmosphere in a family is to a large extent a function of the quality of the relationship *between the parents*; that is, the more positive and warm the interaction, the better the family ambience. The relationship between the parents of children who display deviant behavior often leaves much to be desired.

The interaction *between parents and children* emerges as another important factor. It appears that deviant children do not enjoy good relationships with their elders and do not care about what the latter might think of them. This poor level of interaction directly relates to their deviant behavior.

The literature on deviancy in children traditionally has considered the influence of the mother as paramount. More recently, it has been discovered that paternal influences to a large extent determine whether children display deviant behavior. Deviant children often report disturbed relationships with their fathers, who, in their opinion, are failing in their child rearing. The significance of the role of fathers to deviant behavior in children is that children learn how to behave independently, to adjust socially and to build contacts outside the family particularly through their relationship with their fathers.

The situation is less clear with respect to *dominance*. It is often found that fathers of deviant children are very domineering, whereas the mothers are rather permissive. Frequently, as they get older, the children no longer accept the domineering attitudes of their fathers, particularly if their mothers do not support the behavior of their partners.

Sibling relationships also play a role in deviant behavior because the children of a family tend to interact a lot, particularly when they are close in age. They provide each other with advice and support, help each other with concrete problems (e.g., homework or lending money or clothing) and sometimes unite against the parents in various coalitions. It is therefore not surprising that children involved in deviant behavior often have brothers or sisters with similar inclinations.

Child Rearing

Warm Child Rearing

If one examines the child-rearing model presented in the previous chapter, it will be obvious that warm child rearing is probably the best way to prevent deviant behavior. Warmly raised children generally experience healthy personality development, which means that they are less likely to feel frustrated in life and therefore can cope well when faced with problems. Furthermore, they are quite capable of building and maintaining social relationships, which furthers their social adjustment.

Last but not least, their good relationship with their parents leads them to adopt their elders' norms and values, which normally is an excellent safeguard against deviant behavior.

Cold Child Rearing

In cold child rearing, children experience their parents as being, at the least, indifferent and sometimes even hostile. This cold relationship is usually mutual because the children tend to be indifferent toward their parents, turn their backs on them or even turn against them. This restricts identification and the transference of norms and customs.

The parents have little control over their children. They are not able and often not willing to deal with their children's deviant behavior and respond to it adequately. In cold child rearing, one finds young children with all sorts of deviant behavior and other problems, such as feeding difficulties, bed wetting, attention seeking and so forth. Also, later on in life, coldly raised children are over-represented in all areas of deviant behavior.

While cold child rearing usually precedes deviant behavior, the reverse may also be true. Child deviancy may decrease the parents' love and affection for their children. Although parents may disapprove of their youngsters' deviant behavior, they usually still accept them. Sometimes, however, the behavior may cause such an interpersonal distance that the parent-child relationship is intrinsically damaged. In some cases, the parents merely give up, whereas in others they deliberately distance themselves and evict the child.

Dominant Child Rearing

Dominantly raised children in principle will cause few problems because they have been taught to conform. However, at the same time, they have insufficiently learned to form their own opinions, assume responsibilities and be autonomous. They may run into trouble if they have to act independently, a behavior that may make them feel uncomfortable. Under such circumstances, they are often inclined to "follow the crowd." This means that they have little resistance against deviant influences, should these be present in the groups with which they associate. Because they tend to submit to the authority of dominant people, they may be overwhelmed by deviant peers. Parents may be surprised that their "good" children turn so easily to deviant behavior under the influence of "bad" friends.

It often happens that children try to escape from the restrictions of an extremely dominant child-rearing regime and go their independent way. This frequently causes problems because they have never learned how to be independent. They may experience an identity crisis, with a possible result that they—as a reaction to their restrictive child-rearing experiences—choose a deviant identity. In some cases, such youngsters become completely lost and do not care about anything or anyone.

Permissive Child Rearing

Deviant behavior is often found in children from families where the parents—especially the mother—subscribe to a permissive approach. Permissively raised children usually know how to find their way in life; they are active, sociable and take initiative. If child rearing is too permissive, however, they do not learn to meet any demands or exert themselves, which leads to superficiality, laziness and opportunism. Generally, these are children who have trouble giving direction to their lives. They have never learned to follow rules and be considerate of others. Therefore, they lack constraints on their deviant behavior.

The manner in which parents respond to the deviant behavior of their children is of utmost importance. Their reaction has to be consistent because, if they are inconsistent, their children may develop positive as well as negative associations with deviancy. This may lead to an ambivalent attitude toward the behavior, and the youngsters may become confused and develop a sense of "learned helplessness." However, it is also possible that a positive evaluation of deviant behavior results. If a child has had positive as well as negative experiences with deviant behavior, the overall balance may be positive because positive experiences tend to be better remembered than negative ones.

Generally, deviancy increases if the parents tolerate the behavior or fail to do much about it because the children learn they can act deviantly without fear of punishment. They will feel supported and may behave in deviant ways in other situations. They may even adopt deviancy as a way of life.

On the other hand, a very strict child-rearing policy has also been found to encourage the incidence of deviant behavior. It has been noted that severe punishment is not a good means to prevent or curtail deviant behavior. For a number of reasons, severe punishment often has reverse effects—increasing deviancy. As has been discussed in a previous chapter, severe punishment frustrates children, renders them insecure, may elicit undesired tensions and sometimes acts as an example of aggression. The most that children learn from severe punishment is that they should not misbehave in the presence of their parents. They may compensate for this elsewhere.

Alienation, Avoidance and Escape Behavior

Alienation

Children who grow up in families that suffer from the above-discussed shortcomings may gradually realize that the family is not a very rewarding place. They do not feel at home any more and experience a kind of alienation. As a consequence, they devote less time and energy to the family, their relationships with other family members become less intense, they distance themselves from the norms and customs of the family and—most importantly—their affective ties with the others weaken. As part of this alienation process, the children may demonstrate avoidance and escape behavior.

Avoidance Behavior

Avoidance behavior may take various forms and may be adjusted or maladjusted in nature. Examples of the latter include aggressive behavior, juvenile delinquency and running away.

Avoidance behavior may be expressed in a passive, active or reactive manner—or in a combination of these three forms. In *passive avoidance behavior*, children basically withdraw from the family situation and ignore what is going on around them. They may turn inward and display covert deviant behavior (e.g., theft at home) and clinically maladaptive behavior (e.g., depression, psychosomatic complaints, nutritional deficiencies and suicide). In *active avoidance behavior*, children try to make the best of their life situation, either inside or outside of the family context. More overt forms of deviant behavior accompany this. Characteristically, the youngsters begin experimenting with activities that actually belong to the adult world (e.g., alcohol and drug use, gambling, sex, staying out late, or joy riding). *Reactive avoidance behavior*, aimed directly at the parents, may take the form of harassing and embarrassing the parents, often through a variety of different misbehaviors.

Which form of avoidance behavior children adopt for themselves depends on a number of factors, including gender and personality characteristics. Boys often opt for active avoidance behavior, whereas girls tend to choose passive forms. Extroverts tend to take an active approach, while introverts choose a passive form. Moreover, modeling plays a role—in the present society, children are exposed to a multitude of good and bad examples, so they have lots of choice.

Escape Behavior

Avoidance behavior usually goes with escape behavior. In escape behavior, the children increasingly locate their interests and activities outside the family. They are home less often and seek the company of others with a similar frame of mind. Usually, these others are peers and friends, but they also may be members of particular institutions, organizations, religious groups or subcultures.

Alienation precedes deviant behavior, which in turn may increase alienation. Children often commit deviant acts as members of peer groups or subcultures that adhere to deviant norms and activities and that in a variety of ways criticize parents. This creates distance between youngsters and their parents. Moreover, deviant children eventually realize that their behavior is not compatible with the norms and customs of their elders. They begin to understand that they have crossed the line and are involved in activities that are unacceptable to their parents. This also creates distance.

On the other hand, the parents' attitudes may contribute to alienation. Many parents attribute their child's deviant behavior to external causes, such as the infamous "bad friends." However, some parents ultimately cannot deny that their children are directly responsible for their deviant behavior. These parents then often differentiate between "deviant behavior" and "being deviant." They blame their children for their deviant behavior but do not ascribe a deviant identity to them ("My son steals, but that does not mean that he is a thief, does it?"). In cases of severe and prolonged deviant behavior, however, the possibility exists that parents and others will start labeling their children as deviant, with all the stereotyping associated with such a designation. This creates further alienation. Moreover, if the children identify themselves with the deviant identity assigned to them by the labeling process, they will develop a deviant self-image. This self-image, as a self-fulfilling prophecy, will increase their alienation and make them more susceptible to deviant behavior.

Thus, deviant behavior is not only caused by alienation from the family but also contributes to this state of isolation.

AGGRESSION

Aggressiveness and Aggression

Every day the public is inundated with expressions of aggression in many different forms and degrees. Day after day, the television screen is filled with news of horrible acts that reach the living room from all over the world. Movies and television programs that show rampant aggression receive high ratings. Furthermore, aggression is often the order of the day in newspaper reports. Crimes are thoroughly described to the most minute details. The aggression often concerns not only war and repression, often in distant countries, but also individual cases of abuse and violence that are sometimes dangerously close. A large segment of society does not feel safe and exhibits a general feeling of discontent about aggression and violence.

In everyday life, one may also observe all kinds of aggressive behavior. Abuse and confrontations are already prevalent in young children. Adults usually approach it in more subtle ways. It is not necessary to express aggression by fighting or other kinds of violence—slander, gossip and obstructing others are alternative approaches.

A distinction must be made between *aggressiveness* and *aggression*. *Aggressiveness* is a personality characteristic, a latent tendency to behave more belligerently than most people. Aggressive individuals perceive people and situations as evoking aggression and habitually react in an aggressive manner.

Aggressive individuals assume an egotistic stance in life, tolerating little and having little consideration for other people. They have limited empathic abilities and therefore have trouble attaching themselves emotionally to other people. They are suspicious and jealous, sometimes bitter and revengeful. They often quarrel with people around them, especially children with their parents. It is not easy to raise these children, particularly because the word *obedience* seems to be foreign to them.

Aggression, on the other hand, is behavior that may be caused not only by an aggressive personality but also by other factors. Much aggression is committed by people who in terms of their personality are not very aggressive. Aggression often happens when a situation is out of control because of group influences, especially when the situation involves youngsters.

Aside from inborn factors, aggressiveness is for a large part the result of a learning process that begins in early life. In other words, people act aggressively in particular situations because they have learned to do so, and because they did not learn to behave non-aggressively under those circumstances. Child rearing plays an important role in this learning process. During child rearing, children learn to distinguish between situations in which aggressive behavior is successful, accepted or even approved of by others and situations in which it is not. That many people only know to respond aggressively in certain situations may indicate a deficiency in their child rearing.

The Family and Child Rearing

Aggressive children often come from disharmonious families in which there are many conflicts. Anger, irritations and disagreements are expressed in behaviors, such as fighting, blaming others and shirking responsibilities. This is an unfavorable family situation. The result is alienation, followed by avoidance and escape behavior. The children look for happiness outside the family, first among peers and friends.

In *warm child rearing* situations, children have little reason to develop aggressive tendencies. The positive relationship these children have with their parents usually leads to good relationships with other people. Consequently, they do not often get into conflict with others. Furthermore, because of the positive personality development that results from such a child-rearing approach, warmly raised children cope well with frustration.

Children on the receiving end of *cold child rearing* practices who lack warm ties with their parents are more likely to develop into aggressive individuals. Because of the large interpersonal distance that exists between parents and children, the parents have little control over their children. As a result, the latter are not taught how to deal with aggression in general and their own aggression in particular. Academic literature devotes a lot of attention to child aggression as a result of cold child rearing, particularly by mothers. However, it must be noted again that aggression in boys often is related to a coldness in their fathers.

Parents who opt for *dominant child rearing* may believe that they are setting a good example and teaching their children useful rules for behavior. Yet, dominant child rearing often fails to produce the favorable outcome that parents expect. Children who grow up under the restrictions of a dominant child-rearing regime may never learn how to be independent individuals. Even as adults, they will be dependent persons who do not know how to adapt adequately. People who have been raised dominantly are often faced, later in life, with circumstances they cannot handle on their own. They have not learned to improvise in situations for which their parents have never prepared them. In such cases, they tend to resort to aggression because they do not understand other people's more lenient adherence to rules and regulations.

In *permissive child rearing*, parents do not consistently disapprove of aggressive behavior in their children. Thus, the parents do not provide the children with checks and balances for their aggressive acts. If parents do not sufficiently disapprove of or discourage aggressive behavior, children may interpret this as tacit approval, which then leads to a learning process in which they may adopt aggressive behaviors.

That aggressive parents often have aggressive children may in part be explained by hereditary factors. However, imitation, whereby the parents serve as role models, also plays an important role. Children tend to imitate the parents' behavior and therefore also their aggressiveness. Fathers in particular serve as models for aggressive behavior.

The way that parents react to their children's aggressive behavior varies from case to case. Often families do not discuss aggression at all and subject it to strict, forbidding rules. As a result, the children have no opportunity to come to terms with their aggressive tendencies. Aggression often is severely punished. However, punishment only discourages children from openly displaying aggression in the presence of their parents, and they may compensate for this when the latter are absent. Severe punishment may be counter-productive, causing the child to feel frustrated and in turn leading to aggressive behavior. Furthermore, severe punishment by parents may, in so far as it is aggressive, serve as an example for aggression.

Once children have learned to behave aggressively in a certain way, they will also behave aggressively in other ways. For instance, if children watch an adult commit physical aggression, they may not only imitate this behavior but also show more verbal aggression (e.g., name calling).

Generally boys are more aggressive than girls, especially concerning more overt forms of aggression. Girls are not easily tempted to be aggressive because their sense of self-worth is not as vulnerable and they are less status- and achievement-oriented. They also are better able to cope with frustration. Therefore, they are less likely to get into conflict with others.

The reason for this gender difference must be sought in environmental as well as biological factors. Child rearing, in particular, contributes to this dissimilarity. Fathers are generally more aggressive than mothers, and they also allow more aggression than mothers. Because boys identify relatively more with their fathers than do girls, they tend to become more aggressive.

As noted before, these gender differences relate to the different roles that society expects of men and women. Men supposedly are brave, active and persistent—one expects initiative and achievement from them. Women are more quiet and gentle; they seek harmony and are better able to adapt. Because of these role expectations, society expects and permits men and boys to behave more aggressively than women and girls. Women more often resort to indirect and verbal aggression. This gender difference can already be observed in very young children.

The role differences between men and women and between boys and girls also explain why in families in which the father is in charge of child rearing, the children, especially the boys, tend to be more aggressive. In cases in which the mother is the central figure, the children, particularly the boys, are less aggressive. Boys from families in which the father is absent are less aggressive than boys from complete families. The explanation for this is that they lack an aggressive father model. Girls from such families, on the other hand, tend to be more aggressive than other girls. Perhaps in such families, the mother tries to compensate for the absence of the father by playing his role, including acting more aggressively. Because girls identify more with their mother, they also adopt her aggressive attitude.

It is often assumed that aggression in children can be treated by providing them with harmless opportunities to discharge their aggressive energy through acceptable channels. Because every aggressive behavior uses energy, the need to behave in this manner theoretically should decrease after the child has expressed the aggressiveness and other acting out behavior through activities such as boxing, wrestling, football or soccer. However, research findings concerning this approach are contradictory. Some investigations support the idea that the need for aggression decreases after aggressive behavior, but others indicate just the opposite.

So how should parents handle aggressive behavior in child rearing? Is it advisable to let children vent their aggression? The answer to this question is complicated. If children show signs of inner tension, it may indeed be useful to give them the chance to vent their frustrations, thereby preventing an explosion. Parents should realize, however, that the resulting relaxation will only be short-lived and that their children will not be less aggressive as a result. Parents should further understand that if they allow their children to act out aggressively, this will too readily be interpreted by the latter as approval of the behavior, which will then be repeated. In that case, the situation could go from bad to worse.

JUVENILE DELINQUENCY

Juvenile Delinquents

Young children display relatively few delinquent behaviors. However, around the age of twelve, a dramatic increase in delinquency occurs. It peaks and subsequently declines when the children are approximately sixteen to seventeen years old. At that age, adolescents are faced with adult responsibilities and their opportunities to achieve status by legitimate means are expanding. Thus, juvenile delinquency is typically age-related. It is a transient form of criminal behavior that most children, but not all, outgrow. Adult delinquents, particularly those involved in serious crimes, usually began their criminal career at an early age.

Juvenile delinquency consists mainly of relatively mild forms of criminal behavior, such as breaking and entering, shoplifting, purse snatching, joy riding, theft of bicycles and car radios, and theft from vending machines and parking meters. Vandalism, such as soccer hooliganism, writing graffiti and setting fire, is also prevalent. Serious physical abuse is hardly ever involved, but children often abuse each other through threats, quarrels and fights. Traffic offenses committed by youngsters are often the result of showing-off behavior in combination with the use of alcohol. Relatively speaking, juveniles do not often commit sexual crimes.

There is a clear gender difference in juvenile delinquency. Boys are more active juvenile delinquents than girls. Boys are often involved in aggression and violence (e.g., abuse or robbery with assault), whereas girls tend to commit less violent crimes (e.g., shoplifting).

The reasons youngsters get involved in criminal behavior are in part the same as those that motivate older people. However, some causes are specific to the young and related to their level of development. Youngsters look for what is new and are curious; they want to explore the world and are attracted by anything unusual. They experiment and explore limits. This, together with the need for action so characteristic of the young, sometimes leads them to lose sight of what is acceptable in society. Furthermore, youngsters hate boredom and prefer to be busy. Often, their criminal behavior starts as a game or sport, as entertainment. Added to this is the tendency of many children to look for excitement and sensationalism. They often seek immediate thrills and deliberately look for risks. Much of the criminal behavior of juveniles takes place in groups. The need to impress friends and peers is an important motive that leads many to show off in a variety of ways.

Thus, juvenile delinquency frequently is impulsive in character, causing youngsters to behave without balancing the pros and cons and considering the possible consequences.

The Family and Child Rearing

Juvenile delinquents often come from disharmonious families. They have frequently been exposed to inconsistent child rearing, particularly by their fathers. Generally, delinquents have experienced severe punishments, some in response to their unacceptable activities. The children do not always regard the disciplinary actions of their parents as fair. They feel they have been treated badly relative to their siblings.

As we have discussed, children from disharmonious families often have trouble with interpersonal relationships and identifications. As a result, they become alienated from the family, and in many cases, this leads to avoidance and escape behavior. Passive forms of avoidance behavior usually involve individual covert criminal activities (e.g., theft); whereas active forms may consist of public delinquency (e.g., vandalism or assault), often in groups and under the influence of alcohol. Reactive forms, aimed directly at the parents, may be expressed in a variety of criminal behaviors. Escape behavior often consists of children looking for greater contact with peers and friends. Whether criminal behavior will be involved depends on the attitudes these companions hold toward delinquency.

We have suggested several times in preceding chapters that parents influence the behavior of their children by their example. This also applies to delinquency because children can learn from criminal models. Although delinquent parents as a rule go to great lengths to keep their behavior hidden from their children, some do not. Children who imitate their parents' delinquency do not always limit themselves to that particular type of misconduct but also incorporate other kinds of delinquent behavior into their repertoire.

As has been discussed, children raised in a *warm* manner develop close relationships with their parents. They follow their example, internalize their norms and imitate their customs. Because most parents behave in an adjusted manner, most children tend to do the same. Their parents, acting as representatives of society, have taught them what is acceptable and how to behave according to societal rules. Moreover, because of the closeness between parents and children, the parents are in a good position to keep an eye on their charges and take corrective action, should this be necessary. The children, on their part, are more open to this attention and will respond more readily to measures their parents take.

In *cold* child rearing, children and parents are not very close, and the children do not learn to adapt to conventional norms and customs. Delinquents often report that their fathers especially failed in their child rearing and that they received insufficient warmth from them. Children raised in a cold manner acquire their norms outside the family, mainly from peers and friends. The latter generally are less concerned about delinquency than the average parent.

Children raised in a *dominant* manner usually follow the rules and in principle are not involved in juvenile delinquency. If they are, it is usually at a later age. Nevertheless, dominantly raised children are not very independent and are open to other's influences, including those of delinquent friends. They fit in well with the rather dominantly structured groups often formed by juvenile delinquents (e.g., youth gangs).

Children generally will adopt the rules set by the parents and live according to their norms. *Permissive* parents, however, have few norms and even fewer demands. Thus, their children live in a vacuum and often do not know how to respond appropriately. With dominance, the problem is that children adopt the rules of the parents in a inflexible way and that they may discard these at any moment. With permissiveness, the difficulty is that these rules are not even available. The main connection between permissive child rearing and juvenile delinquency is that permissively raised children never learn to follow rules and be considerate of others. It is remarkable that they often participate in juvenile delinquency at an early age and are more likely to get in trouble repeatedly. The influence of delinquent friends tends to be considerable.

Parental supervision of child behavior very much inhibits the development of juvenile delinquency. Because children spend a great deal of their time outside the family, providing such supervision is not an easy task. However, this task is an important one because a direct relationship exists between juvenile delinquency and the amount of time children spend away from the family. For parents to exercise a certain degree of control over the behavior of their children, they must know where their youngsters are and what they are doing. In this respect, it is striking that many parents of delinquent youngsters are unaware of their children's activities and interests.

The way that parents respond to delinquent behavior is also of great importance. They may disapprove of certain behaviors, counsel their children against contact with certain peers or disapprove of other youngsters' behavior. The latter approach permits them to communicate that certain behaviors are unacceptable and at the same time warn them against contact with delinquent peers. If their children accept this advice, they will not only put an end to the behaviors in question but also avoid contact with delinquents.

Parents of juvenile delinquents often do not actively intervene at the right time with the right measures. Some parents take almost no action against unacceptable behaviors. For example, they ask no questions when their children come home with goods that they obviously cannot afford on their own. Others tend to rationalize ("My child did this because he was forced by delinquent peers") or cover up what their children did ("My child could not have done that because he was at home with me when it happened" or "My child did not steal this, I gave it to him as a present").

The relationship between parental supervision and delinquency appears particularly important in older children. Parents, by necessity, supervise younger children rather closely but vary in the amount of surveillance they exercise over older children. Of course, adequate supervision does not necessarily guarantee that the children will avoid delinquency, but it does increase the chances of it not happening.

RUNNING AWAY

Runaways

Although parents and children have their disagreements, they usually get along well. Children tend to identify with their parents, adhere to the same norms and values and have similar interests and hobbies. Of course, this does not mean that no problems exist in the parent-child relationship. There are disagreements, particularly with respect to leisure activities, music, appearance, clothing, money management, school, chores and the choice of television programs. However, these differences very seldom lead to major conflicts between parents and their children. Generally, children are quite contented in the family.

Notwithstanding these positive circumstances, some children run away from home. They are so alienated from the family that they do not feel at home any more and expect that they will be more comfortable elsewhere. This perception may be accurate or mistaken; whatever the case, it affects their behavior.

More girls than boys run away from home. This behavior usually concerns children between the ages of twelve and eighteen years, with a peak between the ages of fifteen and seventeen. Children younger than twelve usually defer to the wishes of their parents concerning place of residence, whereas those over eighteen generally are regarded as capable of deciding for themselves where they wish to reside. When the latter leave home without parental consent, they are not regarded as runaways.

It has been estimated that approximately two percent of the children between the ages of twelve and eighteen run away from home each year. This estimate may be conservative, however, because parents do not report many incidents and many runaways are not known to support agencies.

Children generally do not run away without good reason. Usually, there are long-standing problems, although some children run away on the spur of the moment. Even though running away normally is the end product of a long process, the act itself is often impulsive, instigated by one final incident. Many children run away without taking identity papers and sufficient clothing and without thought of the possible consequences.

Most runaways eventually return to their parental home. Others find shelter elsewhere (e.g., with a boy or girl friend or with family or other friends) or start living on their own. Some runaways, however, do not find another place and join the ranks of the homeless.

The Family and Child Rearing

The most important difference between runaways and other children is that the former have had more serious and frequent arguments with their parents. Because of this poor relationship with their parents, they are often raised more strictly, which is the reason many runaways cite for running away. In any case, running away is preceded by alienation from the parents, and this alienation leads to avoidance and escape behavior. Running away, of course, is a form of escape behavior.

Another cause of running away is inconsistent child rearing. In such cases, children may become confused about what to expect and may become insecure. In those situations, running away may be intended as a signal to the parents. The child runs away not to stay away but to find out what the parents' real feelings are.

Warmly raised children get along well with their parents and as a result tend to like being at home. They know that they can rely on their parents in good times as well as bad and that they will receive the parents' support whenever they encounter problems. They have few conflicts with their elders, and there is little reason for them to run away from home.

Many runaways blame their behavior on *cold* child rearing practices. They think that their parents do not care enough about them, or they experience them as distant, indifferent and unconcerned. The children do not feel accepted but rather think that they are rejected and ignored. They lack a sense of togetherness and solidarity. The runaways accuse their parents of shirking parental responsibilities. Some blame this on their parents' being too caught up in their own affairs (e.g., job, hobbies). It may be that they treat their children well in a material sense by giving them everything their heart desires, but this is no compensation for the deficiency in understanding and affection.

In more extreme cases, the children experience the attitude of their parents as not just indifferent but hostile and hateful. This hostility and hatred may be expressed in belittling, teasing, pestering, humiliation and so forth. Sometimes the children are the victim of disturbed family relationships, which the parents camouflage by using the children as scapegoats for everything that goes wrong within the family. In such cases, situations may arise in which the children, through self-fulfilling prophecy, meet the negative expectations of the family on a more or less regular basis. Under these circumstances, runaway behavior is a very real possibility.

Most runaways have experienced neglect, exploitation, and significant physical violence or sexual abuse prior to running away from home. Such cases often involve unwanted children, of whom the parents want to rid themselves.

Some children run away from home because they are virtually forced to leave by their parents. It may be that the latter take every occasion to tell them that they would not mind seeing them leave ("Get out of here"; "I don't ever want to see you any more"; or "Why are you still here?"). In some cases, the parents—especially fathers— may only wish to assert their authority by saying such things. Although the parents sometimes may utter these words in haste and regret them shortly thereafter, it may be too late and the child may have left.

Some youngsters run away, not because they have a poor relationship with the parents but because they have a need for independence. These children feel that their elders do not grant them sufficient freedom, and they repeatedly have disagreements with them about the degree of independence they should be granted. Of course, discussions of this nature take place in all families from time to time. During adolescence, children gradually evolve from being a child to being an adult—a process whereby they gain in independence and are capable of assuming increasingly greater responsibilities. One aspect of this development is that youngsters want to carry out an activity as soon as they feel they are ready for it. Parents may observe this process and indeed be willing to grant their children greater independence but at a slower pace than their youngsters accept. Thus, it is a question of balance between the children's wish to be independent and the limits set by the parents. If the scale tips too much to one side, there may be problems, which usually can be solved through discussion.

Some children—because of ideas they obtain from the news media, friends and peers—are convinced that their parents are overly *restrictive* and that this hinders them from realizing their wishes and desires. They feel they are not taken seriously and not treated as equals. Disagreements may arise about the time they have to be home at night, the size of their allowance, their friends and so on. This may deteriorate to such a degree that the children see no solution but to run away from home.

Chances of this happening are greater in *dominant* child-rearing situations, where the degree to which children are allowed greater freedom usually does not keep pace with their personal development. When the children rebel, it is usually interpreted as stubbornness, a temper tantrum or is blamed on external influences (wrong friends). Once they have run away from home, dominantly raised children often have mixed feelings. Because of the strong influence of their parents, they often wonder whether they have done the right thing and suffer from feelings of guilt.

Children who have been raised in a *permissive* environment, where there is no close relationship with the parents and where everyone goes his or her own way, usually do not rebel against their parents; but they, at the same time, may not care much about them either. Therefore, they may run away for the slightest of reasons.

These children often run away because of a need for adventure and variety. They want to experience new things and meet different people. They view running away as a game that brings excitement. Often, these children are bored and looking for ways to relieve this boredom. They act impulsively and do not consider the consequences.

Among the children who run away in search of adventure, there are many who do so because it is the "in-thing" to do. Running away in search of adventure often happens on the spur of the moment. External factors, such as fairs, disco-nights, pop concerts and even chance meetings, may play a role. Running away often occurs in groups—one youngster takes the initiative and others join in. Showing off and holding one's own with peers may be a factor in this type of running away. Children who run away in search of adventure do not intend to stay away for long or for real. They usually return rather soon, often spurred on by a reality that turns out to be less exciting and comfortable than the children initially expected.

References

1. DEVELOPMENT OF THE PERSONALITY IN THE FAMILY

- Adelson, J. (1980). *Handbook of adolescent psychology*. New York: John Wiley & Sons.
- Ainsworth, M., Salter, D., Blehar, M., Waters, E., & Wall, S. (1978). *Patterns of attachment*. Hillsday, NJ: Lawrence Erlbaum.
- Altman, I., & Wohlwill, J. F. (1978). *Children and their environment*. New York: Plenum Press.
- Ausubel, D. (1958). *Theories and problems of child development*. New York: Grune and Stratton.
- Belsky, J. (1981). Early experience: A family perspective. *Developmental Psychology, 17*, 3-23.
- Bullowa, M. (1980). *Before speech: The beginning of interpersonal communication*. London: Cambridge University Press.
- Conger, J. J., & Petersen, A. C. (1984). *Adolescence and youth*. New York: Harper & Row.
- Crain, W. C. (1980). *Theories of development*. Englewood Cliffs, NJ: Prentice Hall.
- Erikson, E. H. (1968). *Identity, youth and crisis*. New York: Norton.
- Gardner, H. (1982). *Developmental psychology*. Toronto: Little Brown.
- Gewirtz, J. L. (1972). *Attachment and dependence*. Washington: Winston.
- Gunnar, M. R., & Collins, W. A. (1988). *Development during transition to adolescence*. Hillsday, NJ: Lawrence Erlbaum.
- Hetherington, E. M. (1975). *Review of child development*. Chicago: University of Chicago Press.
- Kagan, J., Kearsley, R., & Zelasso, P. (1978). *Infancy: Its place in human development*. Cambridge, MA: Harvard University Press.
- Lamb, M. (1979). Paternal influences and the father's role. *American Psychologist, 34*, 938-943.
- Lewis, M., & Rosenblum, L. (1979). *The child and its family*. New York: Plenum Press.
- Lynn, D. B. (1974). *The father: His role in child development*. Monterey, CA: Brooks-Cole.

- Mussen, P. (1979). *The psychological development of the child.* Englewood Cliffs, NJ: Prentice Hall.
- Mussen, P. (1983). *Handbook of child psychology.* New York: John Wiley & Sons.
- Muuss, R. E. (1988). *Theories of adolescence.* New York: Random House.
- Nash, J. (1977). *Developmental psychology: A psychobiological approach.* Englewood Cliffs, NJ: Prentice Hall.
- Parke, R. D. (1981). *Fathers.* Cambridge, MA: Harvard University Press.
- Pilling, D., & Kellmer Pringle, M. (1978). *Controversial issues in child development.* London: Paul Elek.
- Rutter, M. (1972). *Maternal deprivation reassessed.* London: Penguin.
- Rutter, M., Graham, P., Chadwick, O. F. D., & Yule, W. (1976). Adolescent turmoil: Fact or fiction? *Journal of Child Psychology and Psychiatry, 17,* 35-36.
- Santrock, J. W. (1987). *Adolescence: An introduction.* Dubuque, IA: W.C. Brown.
- Sprintall, N. A., & Collins, W. A. (1988). *Adolescent psychology: A developmental view.* New York: Random House.
- Steinberg, L. (1985). *Adolescence.* New York: Knopf.
- Van Hasselt, V. B., & Hersen, M. (1984). *Handbook of adolescent psychology.* New York: Pergamon Press.

2. THE CHILD AND THE FAMILY: HISTORICAL PERSPECTIVES

- Aaron, R. I. (1971). *John Locke.* Oxford: Clarendon.
- Ariès, P. (1962). *Centuries of childhood: A social history of family life.* New York: Knopf.
- DeMause, L. (1974). The evolution of childhood. In L. DeMause (Ed.), *The history of childhood.* New York: Psychohistory Press.
- Dijkhuizen, G. (1973). *The life and mind of John Dewey.* Carbondale, IL: Southern Illinois University Press.
- Freud, S. (1910). *Three contributions to the sexual theory.* New York: Journal of Nervous and Mental Diseases Publishing Company.
- Gesell, A. (1928). *Infancy and human growth.* New York: MacMillan.
- Hunt, D. (1970). *Parents and children in history.* New York: Basic Books.
- Kanner, L. (1941). *In defense of mothers.* Springfield, IL: Charles C. Thomas.
- Kramer, R. (1976). *Maria Montessori: A biography.* New York: Putnam.
- Laslett, P., & Wall, R. (1972). *Household and family in past time.* London: Cambridge University Press.
- Locke, J. (1963). Some thoughts concerning education. *The works of John Locke* (Vol. IX). Germany: Scienta Verlag Aalen (Originally published in London, 1693).
- Muller, P. (1971). *The task of childhood.* Toronto: McGraw-Hill.
- Muus, R. E. (1970). Theories of adolescent development: Their philosophical and historical roots. In E. P. Evans (Ed.), *Adolescents: Readings in behavior and development.* Hinsdale: Dryden Press.

- Neill, A. S. (1960). *Summerhill: A radical approach to education*. New York: Hart Publishing Company.
- Rousseau, J. J. (1974). *Emile*. London: J. M. Dent & Sons (Originally published in Paris, 1762).
- Spock, B. (1946). *The common sense book of baby and child care*. New York: Duell, Sloan and Pearce.
- Spock, B. (1974). *Raising children in a difficult time*. New York: Norton.
- Stendler, C. B. (1950). Sixty years of child training practices. *Journal of Pediatrics, 46,* 122-134.
- Sunley, R. (1955). Early nineteenth-century American literature on child rearing. In M. Mead & M. Wolfenstein (Eds.), *Childhood in contemporary cultures*. Chicago: University of Chicago Press.
- Watson, J. B. (1928). *Psychological care of infant and child*. New York: Norton.

3. THE FAMILY

- Adams, P. (1984). *Fatherless children*. New York: John Wiley & Sons.
- Block, J., Block, J., & Gjerde, P. F. (1986). The personality of children prior to divorce. *Child Development, 57,* 827-840.
- Burgess, A. W., Groth, A. N., Holstrom, L. L., & Sgroi, S. M. (1978). *Sexual assaults on children and adolescents*. Lexington, MA: Lexington Books.
- England, B., & Vaughn, B. (1981). Failure of bond formation as a cause of abuse, neglect and maltreatment. *American Journal of Orthopsychiatry, 51,* 78-84.
- Finkelhor, D. (1983). *Sexual abuse: Theory and research*. New York: The Free Press.
- Fullerton, G. P. (1972). *Survival in marriage: Introduction to family interaction, conflicts, and alternatives*. New York: Dryden Press.
- Gibbons, J. A. (1989). Alternative lifestyles: Variations in household forms and family consciousness. In K. Ishwaran (Ed.), *Family and marriage: Cross-cultural perspectives*. Toronto: Wall & Thompson.
- Glick, P. C. (1984). Marriage, divorce, and living arrangements. *Journal of Family Issues, 5,* 7-26.
- Clingempeel, W. G., &. Segal, S. (1986). Stepparent- stepchild relationships and the psychological adjustment of children. *Child Development, 57,* 747-484.
- Hetherington, E. M. (1979). Divorce: A child's perspective. *American Psychologist, 34,* 851-858.
- Hetherington, E. M. (1972). Effects of father absence on personality development in adolescent daughters. *Developmental Psychology, 7,* 313-326.
- Mzrazek, D. A., & Kempe, C. H. (1981). *Sexually abused children and their families*. Oxford: Pergamon Press.
- Ory, M. G. (1978). The decision to parent or not: Normative and structural components. *Journal of Marriage and the Family, 40,* 531-539.

- Polit, D. F. (1978). Stereotypes relating to family-size status. *Journal of Marriage and the Family, 40,* 105-114.
- Snyder, J. J. (1977). Reinforcement analysis of problem and nonproblem families. *Journal of Abnormal Psychology, 86,* 528-535.
- Wallerstein, J. S., & Kelly, J. B. (1980). *Surviving the breakup: How children and parents cope with divorce.* New York: Basic Books.
- Weevers, J. (1973). The child-free alternative: Rejection of the motherhood mystique. In M. Stephenson (Ed.), *Women in Canada.* Toronto: New Press.

4. CHILD REARING IN THE FAMILY

- Adams, P. (1981). The sibling bond: A lifelong love/hate dialectic. *Psychology Today,* June, 32-47.
- Adams, R. (1973). Differential association and learning principles revisited. *Social Problems, 20,* 458-470.
- Bandura, A. (1973). *Aggression: A social learning analysis.* Englewood Cliffs, NJ: Prentice Hall.
- Block, J. (1983). Differential premises arising from differential socialization of the sexes: Some conjectures. *Child Development, 54,* 1335-1354.
- Dunn, J., & Kendrick, C. (1982). *Siblings: Love, envy and understanding.* Cambridge, MA: Harvard University Press.
- Entwisle, D. R., & Goering, S. D. (1981). *The first birth: A turning point.* Baltimore: John Hopkins University Press.
- Falbo, T. (1984). *The single-child family.* New York: Guilford Press.
- Forer, L. (1976). *The birth order factor.* New York: David McKay Company.
- Lamb, M. E., & Sutton-Smith, B. (1982). *Sibling Relationships.* Hillsdale, IL: Lawrence Erlbaum.
- Maccoby, E., & Jacklin, C. N. (1980). *The psychology of sex differences.* Stanford: Standford University Press.
- Maurer, A. (1974). Corporal punishment. *American Psychologist, 29,* 614-626.
- Stagner, R. (1974). *Psychology of personality.* New York: McGraw-Hill, 1974.
- Stillwell, R., & Dunn, J. (1985). Continuities in sibling relationships: Pattern of aggression and friendliness. *Journal of Child Psychology and Psychiatry, 26,* 627-637.
- Terhune, K. W. (1974). *A review of actual and expected consequences of family size.* Washington, DC: U.S. Public Health Service Publications.

5. CHILD REARING AND PERSONALITY DEVELOPMENT

- Block, J. (1982). Assimilation, accommodation and the dynamics of personality development. *Child Development, 2,* 281-295.
- Buss, A. H., & Plomin, R. A. (1975). *A temperament theory of personality development.* New York: John Wiley & Sons.

- Cartwright, D. S. (1979). *Theories and models of personality.* Dubuque, IA: W.C. Brown.
- Damon, W. (1983). *Social and personality development.* New York: Norton.
- Dusek, J. B., & Litovsky, V. G. (1985). Perception of child rearing and self-concept development during the early adolescent years. *Journal of Youth and Adolescence, 14,* 373-387.
- Eysenck, H. J. (1971). *Readings in extraversion and introversion.* London: Staples Press.
- Hall, E., & Schell, R. (1971). *Developmental psychology today.* Del Mar, CA: CRM.
- Katz, L. (1979). *Current topics in childhood education.* Norwood, NJ: Abex Publishing Corporation.
- Maccoby, E. E., & Martin, J. A. (1983). Socialization in the context of the family: Parent-child interaction. In P. Mussen (Ed.), *Handbook of child psychology.* New York: John Wiley & Sons.
- McCrea, R. R., & Costa, P. I. (1986). Clinical assessment can benefit from recent advances in personality psychology. *American Psychologist, 41,* 1001-1003.
- Plomin, R., & Rowe, D. C. (1977). Genetic and environmental etiology of social behavior in infancy. *Developmental Psychology, 15,* 62-72.
- Rollins, B. C., & Thomas, D. L. (1979). Parental support, power and control techniques in the socialization of children. In W. R. Burr, R. Hill, et al. (Eds.). *Contempory theories about the family.* London: The Free Press.
- Schai, K. W., & Parham, I. A. (1976). Stability of personality traits: Facts or fable. *Journal of Personality and Social Psychology, 34,* 146-158.
- Thomas, A., & Chess, S. (1977). *Temperament and development.* New York: Brunner Mazel.
- Zuckerman, M., Kuhlman, D., & Cane, C. (1988). What lies beyond E and N?: Factor analysis of scales believed to measure basic dimensions of personality. *Journal of Personality and Social Psychology, 54,* 96-101.

6. CHILD REARING AND DEVIANT BEHAVIOR

- Ambrosino, L. (1971). *Runaways.* Boston: Beacon Press.
- Angenent, H., & De Man, A. (1989). Running away: Perspectives on causation. *Journal of Social Behaviour and Personality, 4,* 377-388.
- Bandura, A. (1973). *Aggression: A social learning analysis.* Englewood Cliffs, NJ: Prentice Hall.
- Brennan, T., Huizinga, F., & Elliott, S. S. (1978). *The social psychology of runaways.* Lexington: Lexington Books.
- Burchard, J. D., & Burchard, S. N. (1987). *Prevention of delinquent behavior.* Beverly Hills: Sage.
- Donovan, J. E., & Jessor, R. (1985). Structure of problem behavior in adolescent and young childhood. *Journal of Consulting and Clinical Psychology, 53,* 890-904.

- Goldstein, A. P., & Segall, M. H. (1983). *Aggression in global perspective.* New York: Pergamon Press.
- Henggeler, S. W. (1982). *Delinquency and adolescent psychopathology.* Boston: John Wright.
- Hersov, L. A., Berger, M., & Schaffer, D. (1978). *Aggression and anti-social behaviour in childhood and adolescence.* New York: Pergamon Press.
- Jessor, L., & Jessor, S. L. (1977). *Problem behavior and psychosocial development: A longitudinal study of youth.* New York: Academic Press.
- Kaplan, R. M., Konecni, V. J., & Novaco, R. W. (1984). *Aggression in children and youth.* The Hague: Martinus Nijhoff.
- Maccoby, E. E., & Jacklin, C. N. (1980). Sex differences in aggression. *Child Development, 51,* 943-963.
- Osgood, D. W., Johnston, L., O'Malley, P. M., & Bachman, J. G. (1988). The generality of deviance in late adolescence and early adulthood. *American Sociological Review, 53,* 81-93.
- Quay, H. C. (1987). *Handbook of juvenile delinquency.* New York: John Wiley and Sons.
- Roberts, A. R. (1982). Adolescent runaways in a suburbian: A new typology. *Adolescence, 17,* 387-396.
- Rutter, M., & Giller, H. (1983). *Juvenile delinquency: Trends and perspectives.* Harmondworth: Penguin Books.
- Spillane-Grieco, E. (1984). Characteristics of a helpful relationship: A study of empathic understanding and positive regard between runaways and their parents. *Adolescence, 19,* 881-888.
- West, D. J. (1982). *Delinquency: Its roots, careers and prospects.* London: Heinemann.
- Wilson, J. Q., & Hernstein, R. J. (1985). *Crime and human nature.* New York: Simon & Schuster.

Index

closed family, 25-26
communal living, 47

D
deviance
  and disharmonious families, 99,
    106, 110
  and gender differences, 108, 110
  definition of, 93
  family and, 94, 99
  general background, 93
Dewey, John, 30
divorce, 41, 98

E
education of parents, and child
   rearing, 52
emotionality, 81-82
employment of mother, and child
   rearing, 54
escape behavior, 102-103, 111,
   114
example, setting an, 70
extroversion, 81

F
family, 12, 19, 35
  first emancipation, 25
  inner-directed, 25
  other-directed, 26
  outer-directed, 25
  second emancipation, 25
  single parent, 45
  violence in, 36
family factors in child rearing, 59
family size, 59, 95, 97
family type, changes in, 24
fixation theory, Freud and, 29
Freud, Sigmund, 29

G
generation conflict, 17

I
income of family, as a factor in
   child rearing, 53
incomplete families, 97
industrialization, 25
introversion, 81
intuition versus objectivity, 63

J
juvenile delinquency, 109

K
Key, Ellen, 30

L
labeling, 95, 98, 104
lat-relationships, 46
learned helplessness, 102
learning, 11
Locke, John, 22

M
marriage, childless, 44
maturation, 11
maturation theory, 28
Middle Ages, 20
Montessori, Maria, 30

N
Neill, Alexander, 31
North America, child rearing in,
   26

O
obedience, 105
occupation of father, and child
   rearing, 53
open family, 26

P
parent abuse, 40
parental example, 111
passive-avoidance behavior, 103

Printed in Canada